GREENSBURG
The Twisted Tales
Volume II

Whatever lies before us &
lies behind
Whatever lies behind
us, doesn't compare as
to what lies within us!

Janice Haney

compiled by Janice Haney

Greensburg—The Twisted Tales, Volume II

Copyright © 2009 by Janice Haney
16472 B. St.
Greensburg, KS 67054

Graphic Design & Page Layout by Jim L. Friesen

Printed in the United States of America

International Standard Book Number: 978-0-9819125-1-6

Library of Congress Control Number: 2009925686

In Memorium to those who lost their lives. We will always remember you.

Robert Tim Buckman

Alex Giles

Claude Hopkins

Colleen Panzer

Ronald Rediger

Harold Schmidt

Richard Fry

Larry Hoskins

Evelyn Kelly

David Lyon

Sarah Tackett

Beverly Volz

The following victims were injured on the tornado night and have since lost the fight:

Roberta Schmidt

Max McComb

contents

foreward

May 4, 2007 Many lives have been etched from this date. How do you deter your life from any part of that timeline? How do you escape the phenomenon of the EF-5 tornado of winds over 200 m.p.h., width of 1.7 miles and lasting 29 miles? It has been an experience that'll last a lifetime; one that you do not wish upon anyone else.

This squall has made history in our community, state, and country. You can't erase what happened. There will always be a memoir of the event. Why should we avoid it? We should celebrate that we had so many survivors. It is a miracle that so many lives were saved. The angels were working overtime!

Twenty-one months after the tornado hit Greensburg, I am presented with the task of writing a foreword for, "Greensburg: The Twisted Tales- Volume II." I didn't have any intentions of compiling stories again. But with the persistence from survivors, here it is!

I still have an emotional response from reading the stories. My passion is revealed in putting myself in their shoes. If you took the stories and dispersed them over the United States and asked persons to identify what storm it was, you'd never know they were all from the same tempest. Each resident was in a different place, different situation, and having a different mode of survivorship. The only thing we all have in common is the same time that it hit.

Because we were all put in despair, we all had to make choices quickly in order to start getting our lives back in some order. Others asked why did they not build back in town, why did they move away, why didn't they get the business put back in place? Our lives were put in a whirlwind and we all had to make decisions that were going to meet our needs either immediately or to last us in our lifetime. No one knows what anguish they felt except God. He's the only one who saw their heart aching. Even though many moved, they are very concerned about the restructure of Greensburg. Their hearts will always have a compassion for this town. To those that didn't build back in town but live in the county, they decided to live very close, participate in the communities events and are still taxpayers. They are helping pay for the rebuilding; don't shun those that feed your initiative. It's wise to ask questions than to assume you know the answer.

I'm sure more stories will continue to pop up as time marches on as we all try to get back to "some normalcy" and the town rebuilds. That's where we can all make a note of them and put them in our scrapbooks for the generations to come.

Here is a series of events that have happened since the last book.

Iroquois Center set up for coffee/socializing
Ford donates E85 Escape hybrid vehicle to use ethanol
Groundbreaking for Dwane Shank Motors
FEMA trailers tested for formaldehyde
City Elect Candidate Debate
Boys Basketball team goes to State Tournament
Green Day in Greensburg
Trees from Udall
Knit/Crochet Square Afghans to Survivors
Community Meeting on Green Building
General Election for Mayor/City Council; new Mayor
   & 3 new councilmen
Peoples Insurance Breaks Ground
GM donates 3 Flex-fuel Surburbans to USD 422
5-4-7 Arts Center moved in; 1st LEED Platinum Bldg. in KS
Thronesbery resigns from City Council over Hewitt Contract
Greensburg gets "Make a Difference Day" Award
Week long 1st Anniversary Celebration – Tragedy to Triumph
Sunset Acre Park Dedication
National Weather Service Presentation
Golf Tournament
Business Incubator Groundbreaking
First Baptist Church Groundbreaking
New Water Tower Dedication
Prairie Pointe/Oak View Home Open House
Santa Fe Trail Car Club Show
REO Speedwagon Concert
CBS Early Morning Show
CBS Big Well Park Construction
Care and Share Grand Opening
Going to Town (recreation of Main St.)
Carriage House Community BBQ
Greensburg Cubed Projects
Komotara Apartments Open House
Rodeo Club Street Dance
Community Worship at Davis Park
Community Meal at Davis Park
Farm Bureau Ice Cream Social
Dedication of Victims Memorial
High School Graduation w/President Bush
Candle Light Vigil
Memorial Weekend Tornado Threats
Groundbreaking for Dillon's Store
Farmers Market
Mennonite Housing Authority Homes begin

KW Co. Courthouse being restored
Greensburg State Bank Open House
Greentown Eco-friendly Home Groundbreaking
Masonic Lodge being rebuilt
°Habitat for Humanity Homes
St. Joseph Catholic Church groundbreaking
Kiowa County July 4 Celebration @Mullinville
Historical S.D. Robinett Building being restored
Carriage House Assisted Living Open House
Wilde Flowers groundbreaking
KW Co. Primary Elections
New York Says Thank You Foundation/Barn Raising
9-11 New York American Flag Restored
KW Co Highway Department groundbreaking
KW Co Community Building groundbreaking
Make A Difference Day/Recycling Info.
Teen Center Groundbreaking
Greensburg City Hall Groundbreaking
Discovery Channel/Planet Green 13-part series
Greensburg Trunk or Treat
Light House Worship Center Open House
Greensburg Mennonite Church Open House
Greensburg United Methodist Church Open House
Dwane Shank Motor Open House
Greensburg School Groundbreaking
KW Co. Memorial Hospital Groundbreaking
Peoples Insurance moved in new building
FEMA charges rent on Mobile Home Trailers
KW Co., State, National General Election
Well Done Awards Initialized
Hewitt named Municipal Leader of the Year
Greensburg sends 4 officials to China
10 families moved into Mennonite Housing Authority homes
Dennis McKinney from House of Representative
   to ST. Treasurer
Main Street Mall Money Raised
St. Joseph Catholic Church moved in new bldg.
Streetscape Project begins
Native Sons/Daughters of KS award Grbg w/Service Citation
KW Co. Senior Center struggles for land
Steve Hewitt considers job at Valley Center
BTI/Greensburg moved in new LEED Platinum building
Dillon's store opens new grocery side
Greensburg 1st city in nation w/LEED Street Lights

The above events or actions will be an ongoing cluster as we rebuild together.
Keep the vigor engaged in our chase for a better future for all involved.

a survival checklist

Everyone needs one and in all three areas. Always be prepared for the worst.

Backpack-
Flashlight and extra batteries
Non-perishable food
Bottled water
Knife
Mini First Aid kit
Cash in small denominations
Whistle
Matches
Prescriptions
Important documents: copies of identification,
    deeds, vehicle titles, insurance policies,
    keys to safety deposit box,
Shoes
Clothes
Portable weather radio
Cell phone with charger
Blanket

In Car-
Non-perishable food
Bottled water
Blankets
Shovel
Duct tape

Knife
First Aid kit
Rope
Jumper cables
Flashlight with extra batteries
Pliers, screwdrivers
Toilet paper
Candle with matches

In Home-
Non-perishable food
Bottled water
Candles with matches
Disinfectant
Toilet paper with bucket
First Aid kit
Gloves
Fire Extinguisher
Hand tools- saw, shovel, hammer, screwdriver, nails
Flashlight with extra batteries
Dust mask
Change of clothing
Generator
Ice Chest
Tarp

A big thank you to the persons involved in getting this project ready for Volume II.

To Kathy Senst: A friend that sticks by my side through the ups and downs of life and even when we put together huge projects.

To Bruce Foster: A friend who comes through every time when I need assistance for those most unusual tasks.

To the following photographers who consented to letting me use your talented snapshots:
Stacy Barnes
Joan Hayse
Ken and Mary Jean West
Sheri Taylor
Erica Foster
Ella Mae Marrs
Mary Linenbroker
Lou Tomlinson
Shirley Unruh
Tim Garrett
Bruce Foster

To the Individual Story Writers: who agreed to share your stories for a book that'll be a part of the history of Kiowa County.

submitted by: **CORA BELLE TEBU**

OLD ADDRESS: 612 S. ELM • GREENSBURG, KS 67054
NEW ADDRESS: 404 W. BROADWAY DRIVE • KINGMAN, KS 67068

I Miss Greensburg The Way it Was

My morning started out as usual. I had my breakfast, read the paper and worked on my crossword puzzle. Lois called and I reminded her that I had a hair appointment at 11:30 a.m. so would not be eating at the Senior Center. I also called Shirley Dowell to see if she was ok. I had my hair appointment, came home for lunch and was busy with various duties. Later in the afternoon, I watched game show, Jeopardy, the news, and game show, Wheel of Fortune.

After supper, I searched the TV for something to watch; later I heard that a tornado was heading our way. I was not too perturbed. Soon, my daughter, Karen Bradshaw, called a couple of times to tell me to get to the basement. I called her from there but in my haste, I forgot my flashlight. I remembered that you should get under the stairs. I was putting a chair there, turned back for something else, and the lights went out. That was when the tornado hit. I first heard hail and a bang like something hit the house after which there was a roar which lasted a while.

I groped around hoping to find a chair. I finally found my ironing board and I knew there was a chair close by. I sat for a while but the flashing lightning from the basement windows was so nerve-wracking. I made my way to a bed and laid down for a while. I did hear some banging on my door upstairs but, since it was so dark, I was afraid to try the stairs.

After a while, I heard somebody coming down the stairs with a flashlight. I said, "How did you get in?" He said, "I kicked in your

Debris   *Photo by Stacy Barnes*

front door." It was my neighbor, Wayne Dugger, from across the street. I was glad to go upstairs where I got my flashlight, lighted a lamp, etc. Wayne showed me a lot of the devastation including my double garage that was blown away. My car was at a different angle, awnings and iron railing were gone. My kitchen floor was a mess. The kitchen door had blown open and closed again. There were all kinds of debris on the floor plus a tumbleweed. I had thought when it was daylight; I would pick up that stuff. Another neighbor, John and Cindy Carson, came to the door and told me a lot of the siding had blown off my house, the redwood fence was down, both sheds were hit, etc. The two Maple trees in front were stripped. I lost two fruit trees in the back but a Pecan tree was left standing.

I knew my daughter and her husband would be out by daylight so I settled down for the rest of the night. In a short while, I guess I had dozed, I saw a light in my house. I said, "Who's there?" He said, "It's Arden!" My son-in-law, Arden Bradshaw, and his neighbor drove out. After taking some side roads, they parked on the east edge of town as it was impossible for them to come any farther. On the way out, they had checked at the Pratt Hospital to see if I was there; also checked at Haviland. They walked through all that debris with no light except their flashlights to get to my house; which is in the southwest part of the town. I was really glad to see them. I packed a few necessities as they were taking me back to Wichita. I couldn't stay in my house without water or electricity and we did not know how much structural damage there was.

A neighbor, fireman John Wheeler, had one of the firetrucks there and with Wayne's help, we went to Arden's car. That was when I could see that Main Street was gone, etc. The next day, Sunday, they had lots of calls from relatives and friends regarding me. My brother-in-law in Chattanooga also had calls regarding me.

We were able to go back to Greensburg on Monday. Many were returning so there was quite a line of cars east of town. The devastation was much worse than you could see on TV. We drove around to see more of the damage. Dot Tuttle's house down the street had the roof ripped off as well as the garage. Ed Pooler's house was destroyed. Also, drove by Lois Coberly's; her roof was ripped off but the Cadillac was ok in the garage. Besides, so many homes being destroyed, so were all the churches, etc.

The house where we used to live on 602 S. Oak and my mother's house at 315 E. Grant that Charles and I helped build were gone. The school was practically blown away. I had spent many years there as a teacher and secretary and where my children, Nelson and Karen, had attended. Of course, the Tebu Upholstery place (located where Daylight Donuts was) on north Main Street was gone. It was so sad to see all those other buildings on north Main gone also.

We returned to Greensburg on Friday. In the meantime, a tarp had been put on the top of my house to keep the rain from doing more damage. The car was in the driveway but was totaled from being tossed part way over the foundation of the garage. Each time we went out, I packed two suitcases of my clothes, etc. as well as file folders, checkbook, medicines, cosmetics, etc.

We met with State Farm each time we returned. We were pleased that they took care of all my damage, including the two sheds, cars, house, etc.

The devastation was so severe that it was quite difficult to recognize some of the buildings. Each time we were out, we were able to eat lunch on the Methodist Church lot. Volunteers from many towns brought food which was certainly a God Send for many people.

During all this time, I stayed with my daughter and family in Wichita. Since I could not make my home there and because I do not drive in Wichita, we checked other towns of Cheney, Kingman, etc. Arden had been out to Medicine Lodge on business but stopped in Kingman and visited with a real estate man. He said he had a town home type of place that would be available June 1. It is part of the Kingman Town Homes for affordable housing. We decided that would be the place for me. In the meantime, I sold some of my furniture, gave some away, etc. as there was not enough space in this place for everything. Also, I decided to sell my house and the agreement was that it did not have to be emptied. In the meantime, I had moved to Kingman on June 14. I closed the deal on my house July 25 to Brian Gumpenberger, via Scott Brown Real Estate. That was a sad time for me since it had been home since 1968.

Since Brian is a carpenter, he soon had the double garage back on, new siding, shingles, etc. plus new windows and kitchen cabinets. I was pleased when I heard that Jim and Karen Smith had purchased the house because the Smith family and I go back a long way. It is a beautiful house now and I hope they are happy there.

I have been accepted here in Kingman. The ladies of the Christian Church have given me a big welcome. I have excellent neighbors and I go to the Senior Center at least three times per week to eat. I am an hour closer to my family in Wichita. Since this town is smaller, I do not have trouble driving.

Even though I am an survivor, I feel part of me has been taken away. I am luckier than most because my furniture and clothes were still intact. I still miss my house and I miss Greensburg the way it was. It is going to be a brand new city and they all have my best wishes.

I thank God for my life that he saved and my deepest thanks to my family and my granddaughter, Mira Mullen. Even though, she was pregnant, she was there to help me. Since then, she has presented me with a great-granddaughter whose name is Sadie Belle.

submitted by: **GENE AND JEANIE KILE**
OLD ADDRESS: 504 S. SPRUCE • GREENSBURG, KS 67054
NEW ADDRESS: 10482 W. RIVER RD. • PRATT, KS 67124

God is Good

Friday, May 4, 2007, was a busy day at the Kile residence at 504 S. Spruce, Greensburg, KS. Gene planted his garden that morning of green beans, cucumbers and thirty-four tomato plants. Jeanie was at Debbie Boyles' beauty shop, The Last Tangle, for a permanent. In the afternoon, she cleaned house.

We traveled to Pratt for our usual, "Friday night dinner and Walmart shopping" with Carl and Joanne Schield. We arrived back home at 9:00 p.m. We immediately went to the basement to watch the storm warnings on TV. Soon, it was raining and hailing and the warning whistle was blowing. Just before the electricity went off, the TV weather forecaster said there was a tornado about 1.5 miles wide, 2 miles south of Greensburg and it looked like it was going to be a direct hit.

Gene, our Brittany dog, Jill, and I huddled in a walk-in closet there in the basement. The deafening roar was terrifying. Then a big crash, which was our huge maple tree, uprooted and was thrown through the kitchen ceiling right above us. The sound of shattering glass seemed endless. All of our windows, except one, were blown out. The roof was completely gone and all ceilings, except for part of one bedroom. That big tree blocked the front door and the garage fell in on our car blocking the back so we couldn't get out. We stayed in the dark, dripping basement until daylight. Several friends called in to see if we were ok. We were so thankful the Lord kept us safe!

"Search and Rescue" made us get out as soon as Gene could move limbs so we could squeeze out the front door. Right off, he stepped on a nail that went into his foot. We found a belt to use as a leash for the dog and walked the ten blocks to Dillon's to be accounted for.

We could not believe the devastation we were seeing along the way. Everything on Main Street, except for one building, was completely demolished. When we returned back home, Gene was able to tear the rest of the shop door off and get the pickup out. It was not damaged too badly so we drove to our son's home in Great Bend. Meanwhile, our son, Rick, and his wife, Amy, were searching for us in the Haviland shelters. Of course, our cell phones were not working but Rick finally contacted their neighbor, who told him our pickup was in their driveway.

If it hadn't been for our wonderful family, we probably would've walked away and left the mess. Rick took off work all week. Amy, a teacher, college student grandsons, Micah and Jared, worked two days. Our daughter, Lynne, and her husband, Rick Brunholtz, from Columbia, MO, came and helped for one and a half days. We were so blessed! Due to their hard work, we saved appliances from the basement, dishes, linens, some furniture and most of our wet clothes. We did many loads of laundry at Rick's house and the laundromat. We were so grateful to Masters Cleaners of Great Bend for cleaning many clothes without charge.

Amy and I got to see President Bush while he was in town. He was very kind and compassionate. I received a hug and Amy a kiss on the cheek from George W.

Gene thought we were too old to rebuild so we looked for a house in Pratt. Our doctor, dentist, optometrist and vet were all there. When Gene saw this nice 30'x40' shop and a big fenced back yard, for the dog, for sale, I knew I had a house. We didn't see the inside until later. Like he says, "I bought a shop and the house came with it."

We were with Rick and Amy for six weeks; waiting for the lady to move out. Our kids were so good to us and their wonderful friends brought in dinners for many days and it was great food! Meanwhile, we were hauling our possessions to Rick's garage and storage units.

We were so busy sorting and hauling we hardly had time to mourn our loss. I did real well until later when we drove by our demolished house and saw the huge pile of stone, furniture, cabinets, etc. piled by the curb. That made it final! We had lived in that house 47 years with our kids growing up there. Our friend, Charlie Lance, laid the stone and Gene did most of the building himself. It took thirteen months to finish it. We had lived in Greensburg fifty-six years.

Gene got right back building ramps (Tucker Project, Inc.) for therapeutic riding for the handicapped. He has built eighteen in 2008. We enjoy traveling the U.S.A. to deliver them. We have enlisted Gregg and Mary Anne Childress to help with deliveries.

We loved living in Greensburg and miss it as it used to be. We have adjusted and are happy in our new home. We enjoy our McDonald's morning coffee bunch and our Pitch Club; all former Greensburg people. We continue to attend the Christian Church at Greensburg and are eager to move into the new building soon. God is good and we have been blessed!

Submitted by: CHERYL SCHRADER
202 N. PINE ST. • GREENSBURG, KS 67054

Tribute to Mike

I am going to start my story the day before May 4, 2007. When Mike and I got off work, he from the light plant and I from the hospital, we headed to the courthouse to apply for our marriage license. We were planning an informal backyard wedding at Mikes' mom's house on West Grant on May 20, 2007. We were living at Mike's home on N. Pine St. and I had my house on S. Maple St. rented out. On Friday, May 4th, Mike went to work and I was off. I got the wedding invitations in the mail along with some bills. When Mike got off work, we headed to Pratt to get things for the upcoming wedding. On the way home, Mike mentioned we were going to be in for a bumpy night. I, apparently, didn't see or feel what he did. We got home and got the stuff put away and turned on the TV. We kept watching news bulletins, weather updates … Still I wasn't too concerned. After all, I was home with Mike. I felt safe and secure. When the tornado siren whistle blew, Mike assembled flash lights and camping lanterns. We kept watching the TV.

When the electricity went off, Mike decided to head up to the light plant to see if he could help Chris Kipp who was working. He told me as he left if I heard something like a freight train I should take the dogs and go to the basement. It seemed like he was not gone five minutes when the glass broke and the wind howled inside the house. By then, I was shaking so hard and wondering how I could feel so much wind and hear such thunderous noise inside the house. I couldn't see anything. I went to the door on the back porch which lead to the garage and basement door and couldn't get it open. Now what do I do? PANIC!!! The dogs and I huddled in the bathtub. I still don't know if the tub and bathroom was shaking or if it was me. It doesn't seem like we were held up there all that long.

We got out of the bathtub and I wanted to assess the situation. I immediately smelled gas and ammonia. At that point, I thought the house was going to explode. I got the dogs and we scrambled through the broken sliding doors in the kitchen. I couldn't see much. The carport was gone but the pickup was there. After moving some tin, I backed out of the driveway over whatever debris was there and I headed west. I got to the corner and saw there was no where to go. Wires, trees, debris blocked all roads. I backed up and sat there with the dogs. Our neighbor, Nancy Reeds' brother, Doug, came up to the window and asked if I was okay. I lost it then. The thoughts were nerve racking; where was Mike and was he okay???

The dogs and I traveled over to Reed's and sat and prayed. After what seemed like an eternity, Mike walked up to make sure we were all okay. He was going back to the light plant because Chris was still in the basement. I stayed put at the Reed's. It didn't seem like no time and Mike was back. He wasn't able to get back to the plant due to an ammonia leak. We took the dogs to our house and secured them in an intact bedroom and we commenced walking across town to check on family and friends. We went down Walnut Street. At the corner of Walnut and Grant, I saw Carl Wingfield sitting on the curb. His granddaughter, Mandy from Pratt, had arrived. He was fine. The

apartment building was not so fine. Carl said he weathered the storm down in Jason West's basement. We went west on Grant and got to Mikes' mom's house. She and Gary were okay. Mike's son Lee lived in the next block. That house was gone but Mike got word that Lee was okay from his grandma, Dianne Unruh.

We were told to go to the Dillon's parking lot so we headed that way. I wanted to check on Rex and Shirley Butler and see my house on S. Maple, so we trudged over there. The Butler's were fine. My house was standing but the two – 100 year old cedar trees had been uprooted and were atop the house. We then went back home and Helen and Gary met us there. They had been driving their demolished but drivable Bronco on flat tires. This was about 3:00 a.m. We all tried to get some sleep and we did.

Early in the a.m., Mike's boss Mickey Kendall came by to see if Mike would go to work helping change tires on emergency vehicles. He, of course, did. He no sooner left and some National Guardsmen came knocking to say we would have to leave town; that the whole town was being evacuated. He said we'd more than likely be able to return that evening. This shook me up since Mike wouldn't know where we were but we had to go. The two dogs, Helen, Gary, and their cat and I piled into our Ford Ranger. We stopped at the tire shop to tell Mike but he wasn't there. We left word with Charlie to tell him. We went to the Haviland High School and checked in. That day was a blur to me. Mike and I were once again separated; would he find me?

My friend and co-worker, Mary Lou Brown, caught up with me to say we could stay at her house. She lives just a block from the school. She was gracious enough to let me use her phone to let long distance people hear from me. My cell phone had shot craps. Of course, at the time, I was sure we'd be able to go back home to Greensburg. Finally, around 5:30 or 6:00 p.m., Mike and Kent arrived in a co-worker's vehicle. I was relieved he found me. He had not gotten the message and had gone to Mullinville first (at least he was able to see his son Lee at that time) and then came to Haviland. He had brought a suitcase with a change of clothes and medicine and toiletries. He knew we'd not be going back home that night. So, we took Mary Lou's offer up to stay at her house. She had a house full for sure. Her daughter, Reita, granddaughter, Renee, and her husband and Tuffy and Millie Rush were all given refuge. Helen and Gary went to Pratt to stay at a motel. Mike's brother, Tim and family, had arrived in Haviland to help board up Helen's house. But as ya'll know no one was allowed back to Greensburg until Monday. Sunday, Mike and Kent went back to Greensburg to work for the city. I stayed in Haviland. I meandered around the shelter signing up here and there for this organization or that.

Monday, finally, we were able to go home. Mike and I rode in our pickup and Kent took the co-worker's vehicle. We went to the house and Kent picked up Mike to work. I was at a loss as to what to do, where to start. It was all so overwhelming. Mike was in and out, he got the windows boarded up. Still we couldn't stay in town. Curfew, ya know! So, each day we'd come to Greensburg and each evening we'd go back to Haviland. This went on for two weeks. Finally, we were able to reside at our damaged house, but home nonetheless with no electricity and gas. Rex Butler let us use a generator for awhile. Our intention was to fix the house up, keep my house rented and deal with the aftermath. That was not to be. Our house was in the corridor for the proposed highway and since we had more than 50% damage to the house, we could not obtain a permit for repairs. Insurance money repaired the rental house and we were forced to have the renters move and us move in. It was a very traumatic time for all concerned. Mike continued working for the city each day and tending to personal things after hours. It was a tough summer but we were the fortunate ones that had a house still standing, a vehicle that was not totaled and each other.

Our wedding date came and went but the week after the tornado, I went to the temporary district court in Mullinville and was able to obtain our marriage license. We had finally received our rings. Due to the tornado, they were being held at Fed Ex in Hutchinson. On June 4, one month after the tornado, Mike and I were in Mullinville taking care of business and stopped in to see if Judge Dixson would do us the honors and marry us. She did and so one month from the day came OUR DAY. Our plans were to have our backyard re-wedding on our first anniversary. Well as life unfolds, that didn't take place. We lost Mike to cancer on March 12, 2008.

I would like to continue with our life together as a memorial to Mike. During the clean up months and move, Mike would not feel good; nothing serious but fatigue, sore back, sinus and headaches. We attributed this to stress and working in the elements. November 11th, he was having a hard time breathing so we went to the emergency room. After some lab work and x-rays, he was flown to Wichita. His kidneys had failed and potassium level was dangerously high (which could cause his heart to stop). After some ten days at Wesley Hospital and a battery of scans, probes, and biopsies, he was diagnosed with

cancer; at that time, it was Hodgkins Lymphona. He was released and would have dialysis in Pratt three times a week and would fight this cancer with Dr. Jennings in Pratt. Things deteriorated and he had to go back to Wesley because of a blood clot. That was in December. When Dr. Jennings saw him for the first time, he believed there was more than Hodgkins going on. Before starting chemo, he needed to know exactly what he was dealing with. It turned out to be advanced T-Cell Lymphona; not curable at this advanced stage.

First part of January, he had an appointment with Dr. Maalouf. In his weakened state, the doctor had him flown to Wesley once again. He was given his first dose of chemo during this hospital stay and was moved out of MICU into a private room. I stayed the weekend with him and came home on Monday to work. Things deteriorated and Tuesday he was put on a ventilator. When I got there, the doctor told me that I should contact his family and I did. Mike didn't want the ventilator. He wanted to talk so the doctor agreed to take it out. That was on a Thursday. That night, they moved him to Hospice at St. Francis Hospital. We stayed there a week and they discharged him for home and Pratt Hospice would take over.

Several days after coming home, it was like a miracle. Mike had gotten his appetite back, kidneys were functioning, skin color had improved and he'd get up in the wheelchair to get on the computer. Wow, this was after just one dose of chemo! We began to make plans and had lots of hope for our future together. Dr. Jennings came to see him at home. He was surprised to see him this much improved and said if Mike wanted more chemo, he would agree. He got his second dose of chemo the first part of March. We waited patiently. After the first dose, it took him about two weeks to rally. He didn't make it the two weeks.

I wanted to share our life with you as a tribute to Mike. We may not have had a long lifetime together but the time we did have we endured more than a lot of fifty year marriages. I am saddened we won't grow old together but feel blessed having him with me through the tornado and aftermath.

4-H Pavilion

Photo by Bruce Foster

submitted by: SANDRA PUGH
7200 N. MONROE • HUTCHINSON, KS 67502

Memories of Greensburg

Saturday after the tornado, instead of doing the work I usually do, I was glued to the television all day. I grew up in Mullinville and spent a lot of time in the small town of Greensburg. It is hard to believe what has happened to that little town.

I have so many memories of Greensburg even though they were our arch rivals in all sports. It was where we went when we wanted to go to the movie. I could not even estimate the number of times we walked through the front door of the little movie theater and sat on the left side of the theater in the back row just in front of the cry room to watch the latest movie.

After going to the movie we would drive to the east side of town and get a hamburger, fries and a coke at Sadie's Drive in. She was the first one I knew to leave the peel on the potato when she made the curly fries and they were the best I have ever eaten.

In the summer, we would make the ten mile drive to Greensburg to swim at the municipal pool, and to take swimming lessons. We had many days of fun in the pool getting the required tan.

There were two pharmacies in town, which was amazing for the size of the town. The one pharmacy did not have a soda fountain, but carried lots of gift items. I remember shopping there with my mom for birthday gifts before she owned the soda fountain in Mullinville. I also went shopping with my dad in that little store more than once looking for things for mom.

The other pharmacy in Greensburg was only about two stores north and it had the old fashioned soda fountain which had not changed since it was built in 1917. The fountain was along the south wall, and if I remember right it was the exposed brick wall between the two buildings and was a dark red. There was a large mirror that ran the full length of the fountain. The counter was much larger than the one at the L & R Sundries that I was a soda jerk at a few years later. The man that ran the fountain had been doing it since he was a teenager and I loved to watch him work. I remember walking into the Hunter Drug Store and walking on the hardwood floors. They creaked as you walked across the floor. You couldn't walk anywhere in the store with out them creaking. The whole store was a solid wall of wood, other than the brick wall behind the fountain. The booths were all made of the old dark wood and the backs were high enough that you couldn't see any one in the next booth, and wrapped around the side to enclose you. It made telling secrets easy because no one in the other booth could hear what you were saying.

There was usually a little dress shop on Main Street and I remember one that was just between the two pharmacies. On the south corner of that block there was a little bank. On the east side of the street sat the theater and at one time the library. I remember an insurance company that sat on the north east corner of that block right on highway 54 that ran through the town from east to west.

Behind and just across the alley from the insurance company sat the lumber yard.

Greensburg was always a speed trap from city limit to city limit. But the favorite spot for the local cop to sit and watch the highway then was in the alley between the insurance company and the lumber yard. You couldn't see him when you were coming from the intersection at the only stop light in the town, or from the east when you were going through town. It would probably amaze everyone just how much money that one lone cop brought in for the town each month from that one spot.

My husband and I watched the destruction all day Saturday on the television; we can hardly believe the little town is gone. We have not been able to recognize much in the town, even the highway or the main street. I thought once I saw one of the pharmacies, because it always had a light green tile front. Only part of the façade was left standing. The Hunter Drug Store and Soda Fountain could not be seen any where. The only landmark that we could see was the old courthouse that sits just a block off main, and the elevator that is on the north side of town but near main also. You wonder how they managed to survive, especially the old courthouse, it was only built out of brick.

I have a friend that lived in Greensburg, and on Sunday morning I still hadn't heard if she is okay. I have left several emails with people in Mullinville, Haviland and Pratt to see if they had seen her. She has a sister and brother and maybe she is with one of them, I hope so.

Last night as I looked around the house or opened a cabinet I would catch myself thinking: what would I do if I had to replace everything? Would I remember everything that was in the cabinet or closet to tell the insurance company? If I had the video they tell you to have in a safety deposit box would the bank or box still be there for you to retrieve it.

I have a few sentimental keepsakes from my grandmother and I can't imagine them being gone and never seeing them again. They are scattered throughout the house and I enjoy seeing them as I go from room to room. But … should they all be in one room so they would be easy to get to in case of a disaster.

Grandmother's things are just a few of the irreplaceable things in the house. Pictures and photo albums are also in that category, and how would you protect them in a disaster. I heard that Greensburg had a twenty minute warning to get ready. I would have been scrambling all over the house to try and save some of my favorite items and photos.

My friend loved to scrap book and I imagine she was trying to get some of them and the grandkids who are her constant companions to safety. I hope that my biggest fan is safe and that she will contact me soon.

submitted by: JORDON ELLER

OLD ADDRESS: 118 W. IOWA • GREENSBURG, KS 67054
NEW ADDRESS: 200 S. GROVE • GREENSBURG, KS 67054

We Have Learned to Be Flexible

State Forensics: the event that every drama kid dreams of attending towards the end of the year after months of tournaments, practice, and competition, but I guess things don't always turn out to be the way you expected.

Thursday night I crammed all my clothes and things I needed for the thrilling weekend of State Drama and Forensics. My heart had been pounding all week thinking about how much fun the weekend was going to be and how I really needed to start preparing for some fierce competition. I lied awake in bed for what seemed like hours. My mind just kept racing. So I got up and decided that I better just pick up my room a little bit. Everyone knows how nice it feels to come home to a clean room, where you can just throw down your stuff and jump onto you nicely made bed and just relax. To make a long story short, I finally got tired and went to sleep.

The morning of May 4th, I peeled myself out of bed and just looked around. Man, I couldn't believe I had stayed up that late. I was extremely tired and didn't feel any excitement at all. It was almost like all this excitement had turned into dread. Now I'm not going to lie, I might have even complained and cried a little bit to my mom about going, but you know mom, always encouraging you to go and do your best and she will see you when you get home, then you can crash and sleep. Of course I grab my huge bag and drag myself out the door and walk the half of block to the high school where we were having bag checks and loading the bus for our departure to Salina. I lay in the seat of the bus and thought, "Here we go on an uncomfortable seat... that sun is way too bright, and the sophomores are way too stinking loud for six in the morning." Now I look back and laugh about how much I was dreading to go, but the next thing I knew there was someone yelling at me to get off the bus and get my stuff into our motel room. This is the part where I suppose I yelled something like, "Shut up!" or "No!" Anyways, I moseyed off the bus and got on the elevator, threw my stuff in the room and pulled out my costume for the one-act-play that we would be performing in only a couple hours. Then I was informed that we would be going to the mall to kill some time, do some shopping, or get a haircut to look clean and sharp for tomorrow.

For some reason I got the idea I would let someone that I had never seen before to cut my hair. Let's just say I almost cried when she was done. I hated it. That's all I have to say about it, and I thought, Great … just one more thing to ruin my weekend. I was so mad about my haircut I threw it up in a pony-tail and sat and waited for the rest of the team to finish what they were doing so we could get back to the motel to get ready for the one-act-play. When we got back to the motel everyone was hurrying around and caking stage make-up on as they rehearsed lines. Or should I say yelled because everyone had their doors open yelling back and forth because there weren't enough mirrors in one room. I found it quite humorous. Once again, we cram onto the bus and head to the school. On the way to the school, Mrs. McMurry told us that we would be going to

the opening movie of Spider-Man 3. We were all pretty excited that not only we got out of town, but we get to see one of the biggest movies of the year!

After we performed, we went back and everyone changed into some normal clothes and took off the ridiculous make-up and once again piled back onto the bus. My phone kept sending me weather alerts for Kiowa County, but what's new right? We headed back to the mall. I'm not exaggerating when I say that the theatre was packed. Not one seat was empty in the theatre. When I sat down I thought, "Man, this seat sure is comfortable." Next thing I knew the credits were rolling and I had been told to move so everyone could get out of the row. For some reason I just felt sick all of a sudden. Devin Bundy and I decided to head back to the bus. We were the first ones back to the bus. When we got there we found Marlene Cunningham talking on her phone and she sounded concerned. So instead of going back to our seats we lingered near her for a bit, not meaning to eavesdrop but something didn't sound so calming. "There's a tornado about 4 miles south of Greensburg headed right towards it." Marlene said to Devin and me. I guess I really didn't think anything of it because something like that would never happen to you right? It will go around like it always does and everything will be fine right? So I decided to call my mom. "Jordan, everything is just fine! We are in the closet and I will call you when the sirens go off. We're just sitting here and your dad is out looking at the clouds." Then my mom laughed. And for some reason, this made my heart sink. So I agreed to hang up the phone and wait for my mom's next phone call.

By this time everyone was just getting onto the bus and Marlene informed everyone that the tornado was about a mile out of town. So we all just looked around and Marlene took off for the motel. The feeling on the bus was something that I can't describe, almost like a fear. It was quiet. The bus stopped and we all ran for the television in the lobby.

"DIRECT HIT!" was spelled out in bold red letters across the screen and we just stared, open mouthed, dumb struck. Needless to say, my mom hadn't called back yet. Nobody knew what to do. I mean what could we do? The newscasters kept throwing out random quotes and numbers trying to describe how the town had been destroyed. At first there was one picture they kept showing. "Everything from the hospital to the police station is gone!" one voice said. I cried. Each person on the TV kept saying that a different part of town was hit and I don't think that any of us could even fathom what we were about to come home to.

It seemed like hours upon hours before I got a call from my mom. I tried calling mom, dad, Jess, no one would answer and I was frustrated, but again I didn't think about phone lines and the tower being down. I remember praying. I had never prayed so hard in my life. I saw people cry that I had never seen an emotion on their face. I remember when Alex Reinecke got a phone call from his parents and told us his house had been destroyed along with the car he had been so diligently working on for the last month. All of a sudden I shouted, "DANGIT! I CLEANED MY ROOM FOR NOTHING!!!!" and everyone just looked at me. I guess you have to find some sort of humor in it.

Finally around 2 o'clock my mom called and told me that everything was gone and I remember just crying and thinking how could this be true? I was so relieved to hear from her and find out that everyone in my family was ok, but then she told me that she and Susan just went to pickup Norman Volz and that Beverly hadn't made it. I felt miserable. This had to be a dream, it just had to be.

Still to this day I can't remember what happened after that. The next thing I remember is getting off the bus and running to my mom. I looked over and my two of my friends from Sterling had come to Pratt. I remember feeling Miles' and Jordan's hugs and how warm it felt to have friends that would come all that way just to give me a hug. Miles said he freaked out when he heard about it the night before and tried calling me but my phone had died from trying to get a hold of my other family members to tell them that my family was ok. I don't remember leaving Pratt either, but I do remember my mom trying to describe to me what it all looked like. I just couldn't picture it in my head. Then as we got closer I started to see detours at Havilland that sent everyone else on a different route and we just drove between the detour signs.

We got closer to town and it felt like miles just kept getting longer and longer. Finally, we reached the blacktop and we were re-routed to go around town. The road that we took was the road that goes right north of the cemetery. I remember being able to see the courthouse and how extremely eerie and weird it was, because I never had even noticed it from my house before. I wanted so badly to just go see what my house looked like and I just had to see it for myself.

The next few days I longed to see what was left. Everything on the news was about Greensburg. The pictures and videos were horrifying. It was all one big nightmare. It felt like weeks before we could even get in, but when we did, I didn't cry. We went straight to work salvaging everything we could, but you know the story, I'm sure you were in the same boat.

Now it's my senior year and I'm excited to see what life has waiting for me. At least I have learned a few simple things. The tornado sure didn't make things easy, but I think we all have learned how to be flexible, and how to cook almost anything with a spatula and a spoon. (Lack of kitchen utensils) I have also learned that you can find humor in almost any tragedy such as using the phrase, "We aren't going to let the big bad T-wolves blow our house away!" as a homecoming float. One thing I always do is tell someone they can borrow something only to call them back 5 minutes later and tell them you forgot that it got "tornadoed." Oh and for the record, my room isn't clean. :)

Tornado Debris   *Photo by Stacy Barnes*

submitted by: RYAN CLAYTON
RAPID CITY, SOUTH DAKOTA
GRANDSON OF JAKE AND VELMA KOEHN
NEPHEW OF JERRY AND HELEN KOEHN

Gratitude

The Devastating Tornado
in Greensburg, KS on May 4, 2007

Almost all of my relatives, about twenty-three of them, live in Greensburg. Collectively, they lost ten homes on May 4, 2007. The enormity of this storm and absolute unbiased destruction would have shocked my ancestors that lived their entire lives in Greensburg dating back to the late 1800's.

Being a military brat, I was never as fortunate to grow up in the community my parents were raised in. I can, however, proudly state I remember many wonderful and fascinating visits with my relatives, attending family reunions at the Big Well Park, and getting my daily fountain soda from Hunter Drug. Being trucked around the world and ultimately residing in South Dakota, the appreciation for my family in Greensburg was never lost. The gentle kindness of rural Kansas residents instilled tremendous pride in the only community I can and have ever called home.

May 4-5, 2007, was the toughest thirty-six hours of my life. Not knowing the survival of my relatives weighed heavily on me, my siblings and my parents. We, after all, are only part of a few members of the family not living in Greensburg.

We spent all day Saturday utilizing every last communication device between us, five cell phones and three land lines trying to get word that our relatives were safe. It wasn't until late Saturday evening that we had accounted for all relatives. Relief!

The nonstop media coverage failed miserably to prepare me for the damage of this epic storm. On May 6, 2007, the thirteen hour drive from Rapid City, South Dakota to Greensburg, Kansas, to comfort and care for our family seemed like an eternity. About a mile north of Greensburg, driving south on 183 Hwy, I began seeing the results of the storm; shredded trees, tattered debris, broken utility poles and massive amounts of standing water. Little did I expect to have the dozens of flashing emergency lights trigger the realization that the town was possibly gone.

Monday, May 7, 2007 some of the residents of Greensburg began staging on the corner of 183 & US 54 Hwy. for the long one-mile trek into the city limits. Embraced, tear-filled reunions of friends, neighbors and family began to take place with the visual assurances that the fortunate residents survived.

I didn't fully understand the magnitude of the storm until we were being escorted into Greensburg by several Kansas Agencies including; KDOT, the National Guard and the Highway Patrol to assess the damage and try and salvage the remnants of over a century of life.

I had the privilege to drive and support my disabled Uncle's first trip back into town after he was evacuated some two days earlier. The motorcade began to move, with the first check point verifying residency, writing of your address on the windshield, and offering condolences. The second check point providing disaster awareness information and condolences. The final check point was at the city limits for traffic control. For me, the emotional well had begun to overflow with the one-mile drive into town and became uncontrollable with the breakdown of my uncle exclaiming that he did not want to go back, don't make me go back. I told him I was sorry, but we need to. As we entered the city limits, the first thing visible to the North was a mini-van standing on its nose stuck into a motel, and to the South, a row of destroyed John Deere farm equipment. I had always located my destinations within Greensburg by landmarks and recognizable structures.

For my Uncles house, turn right at the J-Hawk Motel and travel several blocks past the park. On this day, it would be a contrasting trip. I nearly missed the turn as there was no J-Hawk motel to guide me to my turn. We traveled one block, debris and no homes, two blocks still debris and no homes, after three blocks some walls were visible but no homes. Everywhere you looked complete and utter destruction. Homes, businesses, schools, churches, motels, and coveted icons were all wiped away by the fury of Mother Nature. The following 48 hours would add more grief to the town with the discovery of two more fatalities bringing the total to ten. All I could think of was when will it stop?

I wish to send my many heartfelt thanks to the local, state & federal agencies that were there with their assistance in the wake of this terrible tragedy. My hat is off to all of the generous men and women who have contributed in some form or another to the recovery and rebuilding of Greensburg; Kansas Americas Hometown.

My sincere gratitude to the human compassion in the wake of this tragedy.

submitted by: **PAUL AND SHIRLEY UNRUH**
R.R. 1, GREENSBURG, KS 67054

Thank You for Your Help

Paul and Shirley Unruh live 6 and ¾ miles south from the junction of US 54 and US 183, on the west side of Highway 183. We are where the EF-5 tornado went across the highway from west to east.

May 4th, 2007 was a typical day. Up at six a.m., breakfast, then off to school by 6:55. Nothing out of the ordinary happened at school. After school, I arrived home around 4:30 p.m. I quickly changed to shorts and was out the door to mow the lawns. As I was walking out the door, Peter and Haley Kern drove in the yard to pick up the rototiller, as they wanted to work up a spot in their yard for a garden. I checked the rototiller to make sure it was full of gas. Peter loaded the rototiller while Jackson Unruh and MaKenna Kern played on the trailer.

Seeing the John Deere tractor (mower) in the round top, and having to wiggle it to get it out of the shed, I chose to use the push mower. I mowed our lawn first, which took about an hour. I filled the mower tank with gas and headed for my folk's yard. Mowing started on the south end and worked my way around to the north. About 8:00 p.m., I was mowing on the east side when it started to sprinkle. I could see in the south, the clouds were very dark. I knew we were in for a storm. About fifteen minutes later, the mower ran out of gas. Since it was raining, I pushed the mower into the garage.

Inside the house, I showered and put on my pajamas. I also put on a T-shirt and a pair of shorts. Then I headed for the kitchen to read the mail.

Paul came home around 9:00 p.m. in heavy rain. He had been working north of Greensburg with the grader and scraper. Nicole was in the study working on-line on her course from Fort Hays University. She is working on her Master's in Library Media. Jackson, Nicole's son, 19 months was in his bed asleep. Paul went into the study and turned his computer on to get the time cards to pay my mother's care givers. It started hailing, so Paul went into the garage to look outside. He came into the kitchen, where I was reading the Hutchinson News, and said, "the hail is really jagged." Nicole heard him and came from the study and said, "Let me see." So Paul and Nicole opened the patio door. We heard a window break. We all went to Paul and Shirley's bedroom. We could see water coming in on the window sill. Only the outside windowpane broke, but the wind was blowing so hard that the water was coming into the room, I went into the bathroom to get a towel. As Paul put the towel on the window sill, the lights went out. We heard a swish sound, which lead us to believe that the wind direction changed. Paul said, "We need to go to the basement." Paul felt the Lord was telling him now is the time to go to the basement. With flashlights in hand, we started for the basement. Nicole stopped to pick-up Jackson from his crib. Jackson lost his pacifier as they walked out of the room. Paul told Nicole, "You do not have time to pick it up." We made our way down the stairs to the southwest bedroom and huddled together in the closet under the stairs. Paul commented, "The wind picked up and it was difficult to close the basement door." We knew there was a change in air pressure because it affected our ears. Jackson was very

calm until his ears started popping. Paul said he heard a freight train, but I could hear the house coming apart. I heard windows break, boards hitting the walls. When the noise stopped, Paul went to the bedroom door, and looked out. He came back and said we needed to stay a little longer because it was so dirty in the hallway.

We waited a little longer, and then walked out into the hall. There was a beam and 2 X 4's on the staircase. We could also see there was no roof over the stairs. Nicole and Shirley asked Paul to go upstairs and find shoes for them. It was taking Paul a long time finding shoes. Nicole and I were getting impatient. Nicole said, "There are some flip-flops in Austin's bedroom." (Austin's bedroom was in the northwest corner of the house). I kept Jackson and Nicole went upstairs to find shoes for the two of us. Nicole found me a pair of blue shoes, but did not find her a pair, she picked up two shoes, a right and left, and came back to the basement. We put the shoes on and started upstairs.

We are lucky our basement door opened into the stairwell, because in the utility room, the floor was covered with insulation and 2X4's. We made our way over the insulation and 2X4's to get to the kitchen. The roof was gone over the kitchen and most of the doors on the upper cabinets. There was insulation, bricks, wood, and furniture all over. Paul was with us by now and we were looking for a place to get out of the house. We were able to climb over the bricks out the patio door on the north side of the house. We could see that the roof of my parents house was also gone.

On the patio, we looked around the farm and could not see any building. We also had a gas smell. We were trying to figure what we could do. Paul's cell phone was plugged into the outlet in the utility room. As we left the house he picked up his cell phone. He tried to call our son, Austin, in Basehour, KS (Kansas City Area), but could not get out. My cell phone was in the car. Nicole went over the debris to the car to get my cell phone. Nicole dialed Austin's home phone number. It rang and rang and no body answered. So Nicole was leaving a message that the farm was gone. Austin picked up the phone and talked to Nicole. It was not long after that, Paul's cell phone rang. It was Carmen Selzer, Harry and Linette Koehn's oldest daughter from Sharon Springs, KS. She said she knew there was a tornado in the area and she could not get a hold of her parents. Paul told her to continue to try calling them, because our farm was gone. Paul also told her she needed to call others in the family and tell them the farm was gone as we could not call out with our cell phones.

We started walking around my folks house, when we saw a car driving up the driveway. It was a storm chaser, he wanted to know if we were ok. He told us the tornado was headed for Greensburg, so we would not get any help from Greensburg. In the lane (driveway), we could see large tires everywhere, trees uprooted, and wood everywhere. It was hard seeing all the destruction with only a flashlight.

We were trying to decide what we should do for the night. We knew that the bedrooms in the basement were ok, so we could spend the night in those two rooms. Since none of the vehicles we had

had any windows in them, plus there was so much glass inside, we decided it was not a good idea to use them. Soon we saw another set of lights come up the lane. It was my brother, Harry, and Linette's brother, Royce, in Harry's little red pickup.

Harry stated that their farm was ok. Carmen had got a hold of her folks and let them know about our home and the farm. Harry told us we could go to their house for the night. So one at a time he took us the two miles to his house. Nicole and Jackson went first, then Shirley, and last Paul. We ended up staying with Harry and Linette for five weeks. We do appreciate their hospitality and putting up with all of our belongings in their home and shed.

The next day we were up early and ready to go back to the farm to see what we could save. We were overwhelmed when we arrived at the farm. What a mess! How are we going to get all of this mess cleaned-up? Where do you start? Plus, it looked like it was going to rain. With Harry, my brother, and Royce, Linette's brother, we worked on getting items out of the house before the rain.

With the help of many volunteers, we worked at cleaning up the farmstead for the rest of the summer. In February, 2008, we started digging a basement to build a new home. We hope to move into our new house by Christmas of this year.

We are thankful for all the kindness shown by our families. It is so amazing the many connections God has brought about through this disaster. He sent so many volunteers to help clean up the farm. Also, the help from FEMA, Mennonite Disaster, Friends Disaster, Christian Disaster Relief, and many, many others. With the help of family and volunteers, our lives have been blessed as we worked cleaning-up and rebuilding our farm. Thank you for your help.

Paul Unruh House   *Photo by Shirley Unruh*

SUBMITTED BY: A.L. "SPANK" AND RUTH ANN HANVEY
OLD ADDRESS: 623 S. SYCAMORE • GREENSBURG, KS 67054
NEW ADDRESS: 10235 S. STREET • GREENSBURG, KS 67054

The Beauty of a Fresh Start

Looking back on it, the day of May 4, 2007, seemed like such a normal day to us - until 9:45 p.m. when our lives were changed forever. On that fateful day, we got up, went to work, came home, ran errands, cleaned house and went about our normal routines. We didn't have a clue what was ahead of us. My mother had always said that the beauty of life was not knowing the future, or we wouldn't go on. Maybe she was right.

When Spank got home from work at Panhandle Eastern that evening, he said that storm chasers were parked at the intersection of Highways 54 and 183. We joked, wondering if they knew something we didn't. We ate supper, watched television for a while, and then started listening to the weather reports. As the evening went on, it looked like we might be in for a large storm. In thirty years of marriage, Spank has never reacted to a storm other than to go outside and watch the clouds. When we realized a bad rotation was headed towards Greensburg, Spank got dressed. I, on the other hand, thought it would lift or go around us, so I stayed in my sweats and socks. Spank soon said we needed to go to the basement. However, Jack, our yellow Labrador Retriever, didn't want to go. We tried several ways to get him downstairs without any success. Finally, Spank pushed and I pulled the ninety pound Lab down the stairway.

Our younger son, Andy, called and said he was coming home, and we told him to stay where he was in Dodge City. My brother Mark Beckett called from Garden City, and while I was talking to him, my ears popped and I told him I had to go. We walked around the corner into a narrow hallway. I got down on the floor and Spank covered me with his own body just as the tornado hit.

The sounds seemed like they lasted forever. I'm sure they lasted anywhere between 15 seconds and three years. Some people say tornadoes sound like a freight train, but we thought it sounded more like a jet engine...like we were right next to it!

Our basement was fairly intact, but all of the windows were broken out and the rooms were full of debris. Spank went upstairs and had to push the door open, but could only open it a little way. He found a circular saw blade imbedded in the stair framing. While he was upstairs, two more tornadoes came through and he hurried back downstairs again. I said to him, "We are going to be alright, aren't we?", meaning was the house okay? He told me no.

When we decided it was safe enough to go upstairs again, I grabbed a pair of Andy's shoes because I was still in my stocking feet. His shoes were pretty big on me but much better than walking on glass in my socks alone! It was a shock when we came out of the basement. Our house was destroyed. However, we didn't have time to worry about it because we needed to check on our neighbors. We went over to Ronnie and Dorothy Sanders' to see if they were okay. When we couldn't hear anything, we went to Shelby and Bill Waymire's and found Dorothy there. Fortunately, Ronnie had double knee replacement and they still had him in the hospital in Pratt, so he did not have to go through this experience. Spank and I pulled Bill,

Shelby and Dorothy out of the Waymire basement window. I went back to our house and found Bill a pair of Andy's shoes to wear.

While all of this was going on, both of our sons, Matt and Andy, were talking on the phone with each other. Matt, our older son, had asked Andy to call someone in Greensburg to see what was going on. Andy called D. J. McMurry and he said, "Where are you, kid?" Andy told him he was still in Dodge City and D. J. told him that this was good news because Greensburg was gone. Andy decided then that he was coming home. He put his flashers on and acted like he was with the emergency workers headed toward Greensburg. He got as far as the Coastal Mart store on the west side of town, then left his pickup running and told the emergency workers they could move it if they needed to ... or they could just have it! He was going to go in on foot to find us. He ran from that location at Highway 54 and Bay Street to our home on South Sycamore without a flashlight. Later, as we walked back out together, we couldn't believe that he could have done that because it was so difficult walking WITH a flashlight. I can't imagine what was going through his mind as he was coming home.

Matt was stuck in Hutchinson with duties there and was frustrated because he couldn't get in contact with of any of us. Our cell phones didn't work since the towers were down or too far away to reach signal. We couldn't let anyone know how we were and that was frightening for both us and for them.

When Andy got near what was left of our house, all he could see was someone standing in the street with a big yellow dog. He yelled, "Jack!" and we knew who it was. Andy told us the whole town was gone. We decided to walk back to Andy's truck, a journey of a little under a mile. When we passed the Big Well, we couldn't even tell what it was. All of our landmarks were gone. When we made it back to Andy's truck, it was an unreal sight for us. There were all kinds of emergency people working and more flogging into town by the minute. There were many survivors walking around in various forms of dress and all were looking stunned and shell-shocked. While we were standing there at the truck, Gerald Morehead said he needed help finding his wife Lois, so Spank went with him to look for her at the J-Hawk Motel where she was working that night.

We decided to walk back to the house to gather a few things now that we had our bearings a bit. When we did, we couldn't believe all of the damage and all of the water in the streets...was it from the water tower that collapsed or had it rained that hard? After we got back out again, we drove Andy's truck to the Panhandle Eastern Pipeline offices to spend the night.

Little did we know at the time these events occurred, that it would be the easiest time of the whole experience. After finally being allowed back into town, we realized that we hadn't seen anything much in the dark that night, because in the daylight it was a horrible sight beyond words. If it hadn't been for our sons and my brother and his wife, we wouldn't have been able to save anything at all since we were in such a state of shock. Dealing with the insurance companies, the city, FEMA, and all of the paperwork was much worse than dealing with the tornado destruction itself. We have a new appreciation of the Salvation Army. They were there and continue to be a huge source of help to us all. We also appreciate all the help of friends and relatives, the Panhandle personnel, my friends and acquaintances at the Dietetic Association, and many strangers who helped us all along the journey.

Although our home and most of our things were gone, we survived without a scratch. One year and four days later, we moved into our brand new home out in the country and were settling down

again after spending all that time in a metal building. That metal building magnified the sound of that year's frequent storms and was frightening. It is amazing all the little things we took for granted in our everyday life before, and we doubly appreciate them now. In a way it's funny, that after the storm, we couldn't even decide on pizza toppings -- and then we had to turn right around and make so many decisions in the building of our new home. The storm has been both a dramatic loss and a blessing for us. We lost so many things but then gained the beauty of a fresh start in our lives.

submitted by: HELEN SCHRADER

OLD ADDRESS: 518 W. GRANT • GREENSBURG, KS 67054
NEW ADDRESS: 715 S. HIGH ST. • PRATT, KS 67124

Click My Heels Like Dorothy

May 4th, 2007 was a usual day for me. I worked all day at The Big Well. There were clouds in the sky and windy. We always have wind.

In the early afternoon, there were cloud chasers who came into the gift shop. There were storm warnings around Garden City. They were all up beat. As they went out the door, I said, "Hope you don't find any!" Little did I know what was coming.

After I got home from work, we always turn the TV on. Soon, the weather man in Wichita started talking about a big storm gathering around Protection. At first, they cut in on the programs, and then later, they just stayed on.

I rented a garage from Mary Linenbroker to keep my pickup in. We had it at home. I said to Gary, my son, we'd better go put the pickup up; it might hail tonight. So, we did. I had forgotten something at the store and stopped to get that. We can't even remember what we ate for supper that night.

Tornadoes were being spotted all around Protection. We had no basement in our two bedroom house. Around 8:00 p.m., it really started to get bad to the south. The tornado was on the ground and crossing 183 Highway. Then the weatherman said looks like it might hit the east side of Greensburg. We lived at 518 W. Grant. I said maybe we'll be ok. But then, it turned due north and headed straight for Greensburg. We could have gone to Kile's across the street. They had a basement but we didn't.

Then the hail came in big clumps and I said, "We're not going out in that." I thought I would put on better shoes, get my purse, and put the cat in her cage. She has always been afraid of storms and would go hide. This time she didn't do that. She stayed by Gary. Before, you would have had to push her in and shut the door quick. She just walked in. It was still hailing.

I had a fifth-wheel trailer and I thought the hail was going to ruin the roof. But they told me hail wouldn't hurt the rubber roof. The tornado was three miles from Greensburg. The weather man says,

"It's huge, folks, take cover now." Then the electricity went off. Gary says, "Mom, it's here! Get to the hallway! Get a comforter, hurry!" So, we and the cat huddled in the small hallway. When the storm hit the house, I said, "My God what have we done! We are going to die right here!" And I fully expected to.

You could hear the windows breaking, big thuds, and the loud roar of the wind. We were praying so hard. Then after a while, it got real quiet. Of all things, the phone rang. It was my son from Salina. He says, "Mom, are you ok?" I said, "I was but the house isn't. I hear it coming again!" I threw the receiver on the floor and we went back to the hallway. That time, the whole house shook. I'm thinking its going to go for sure. Then it was over. The whole east wall was pushed loose and out. Windows were gone and mud and debris was everywhere. We made our way outside with a flashlight and couldn't believe what we saw. Kile's roof was gone. We could see our neighbors with a flashlight and knew they were ok.

I didn't need to worry about my fifth-wheel; it was destroyed as well as our cars. We had a Bronco II in the driveway. All the windows were out and had big dents. Gary said, "I'm going to start it." I said, "You can't get out!" There were big tree limbs behind it and in front between the carport and it; about three feet high. To get up in the yard, you had to come over a bank. The Bronco started and he put it in four-wheel drive. On the third try, he came over the limbs and up into the yard.

My son, Mike, lived on the east side of town. So, we started out to see if he was ok. We finally got to his house, but no one there. His house didn't look as bad as ours. We had to go back to get the cat and as we drove up, he and Cheryl were walking by. He was ok but worried about his son Lee that lived three houses west from us. He was ok.

We went back to his house and stayed the rest of the night. Early the next morning, the police came and told us we had to leave town. Mike took us to Haviland to the school gym.

We couldn't get back into Greensburg until Monday at noon.

My pickup survived; with a new windshield and side glass we had something to drive. The house was not repairable and was bulldozed down. When I got the insurance money for the house, I bought one in Pratt. I still have my lots in Greensburg; maybe to rebuild on.

Tornadoes are still on our mind. Since the storm, I have lost my son, Mike, to cancer. My husband has been gone seven years.

I still have my job at The Big Well. It has been good for me to meet all the nice people who come by to see the tourist attraction. My husband, Clint, and I moved to Greensburg in 1950. He worked for one of the booster stations for thirty-three years. Greensburg was our home. I wish I could just click my heels together like Dorothy and it would all be back safe and sound.

submitted by: AMY NICKELSON
ONLINE COMMUNITY MANAGER OF THE GREELEY COLORADO TRIBUNE

Resounding Spirit Fills Quiet Little Town

Hundreds of Greensburg residents and Patriot Guard motorcyclists from around the country line Main Street just before the arrival of President Bush on May 4. Bush visited the small southwestern Kansas town a year after it was devastated by an EF5 tornado. A reminder of the storm's power, a twisted chunk of metal, remains lodged in the trunk of the tree in the foreground.

Silence is something usually found in multitudes on the Kansas plains, punctuated by calls of doves and persistent whips of wind.

That silence was broken on May 4, 2007, over Greensburg, Kan., when a thundering EF5 tornado leveled the small burg. It was 1.7 miles wide on the ground, almost as wide as the entire town. The tornado could have easily closed the book on the dying town's future — but it didn't. A year later, the town is dusty, desolate, yet abuzz in its rebirth. With incredible strength, unfaltering tenacity — and a lot of noise — the residents of Greensburg are reclaiming the place they call home.

Earlier this month, a co-worker and I were there to mark the year anniversary of the storm that ate up the place where my father grew up, where my grandparents lived, and where I spent my school vacations getting familiar with the quiet prairie and stoic lifestyle.

As the town began cleaning up in a hushed shock a year ago, a foreign sound stumbled through the empty streets. I heard it as I picked through pieces of my grandparent's house on Garfield Street. Trucks and bulldozers shook the air with a diesel growl as they hauled off debris. It was a haunting sound I had not heard on these streets before.

That rumble has yet to cease. The sounds of construction are as persistent as the wind. But now, it sounds like progress, like lives being rebuilt with nails, boards and iron will. It sounds like hope and excitement, something for residents to rally around besides their loss.

Greensburg is rebuilding "green," a town-wide effort to use as many environmentally friendly materials as it can to bring the town back to life. The effort has been documented for the past year by a crew from the Discovery Channel, which will air a program about Greensburg's rise from the rubble in early June.

A weekend celebration on May 3-4 marked a year's worth of accomplishments for the town that has managed to hold on to about 700 of its residents, most of who still call FEMA trailers home.

National media were in town to document the celebration that included a car show, new building dedications, a concert in the park, community worship service and candlelight vigil to honor the 10 residents killed in the storm. President Bush was there, too, personally handing each of Greensburg High School's 18 graduates their diplomas on May 4. His motorcade sailed down a Main Street lined with hundreds of U.S. flags held by Greensburg residents and members of the Patriot Guard Riders motorcycle group, who had come by the hundreds on rumbling bikes.

Sounds of Progress

Despite national fame, Greensburg's streets are still littered. They hold at their edges twisted metal, broken tree roots bigger than thighs, slabs of forgotten houses. They are ripe with pieces of history that never made it to the landfill.

Now, blocks stretch out full of empty dirt lots where houses used to stand. Gaping holes mark where foundations have been dug out. They look hungry and scary, begging you to peek over their edges and see for yourself what wind can do. I bend slowly, lock my knees and look in on the past as the gusts pick up around me.

But new, green projects are on the rise. The 5-4-7 Art Center is an eco-friendly building encased in strips of glass. I stand outside and watch it reflect the spirit that lives here — fragile but not frail, transparent but strong, built delicately but able to withstand the stones.

The wind carries to my ears the pound of hammers erecting the shell of an eco-friendly house a block away. There is laughter from children playing on the new eco-friendly playground. There is applause as the new, bigger water tower is dedicated.

The wind lifts the dirt from nearby vacant lots, anointing the tower's belly a hundred feet over my head with the same coat of dust that sticks to my boots and covers the legs of my jeans.

Sounds of Persistence

There's one speck of normalcy in Greensburg — the little Kwik Shop on U.S. 54 — serving gas, food and gossip.

The convenience store looks like one in any other town, in any other state, along any other highway. But inside, residents gather to share word of what's happening around town and who's doing it. There are a few narrow aisles full of groceries. This is still the only place to buy food for 15 miles. Here, the scent of fresh fruit smells unusual against the dusty landscape. I linger by the oranges, close my eyes and inhale.

Construction workers fill these aisles, too. They are itinerant laborers in a portable-trailer town, arriving Mondays and gone by Fridays. They bring coolers of beer and cigarettes, along with smells of wood, metal and danger around their edges. Day in and day out, they build, helping turn this noisy, constantly changing town into something permanent and peaceful once again.

They are no different than the rest of us who stop in at the Kwik Shop, travelers and residents alike. Sometimes we are nice, sometimes we are tired and impatient. Some days we are strangers, but on others we say hello in the aisles, like neighbors. It is then, in those smiles and nods, those small connections, when I understand how the people of Greensburg are facing the daunting challenge before them.

Watch. Nail by nail, strangers and friends are linking the past to the future, and slowly rebuilding the spirit within the city limits.

Listen. Outside, the pounding hammers and the persistence of the Kansas wind will hold constant for years to come.

Greensburg, KS, Tornado Facts

1.7 miles
Widest width of tornado as it went through town.

28.8 miles
Distance the tornado traveled.

205 mph
Approximate strongest surface wind in parts of Greensburg during the tornado.

11
Deaths from the tornado, 10 were Greensburg residents.

961
Homes and businesses destroyed.

216
Homes and businesses with major damage.

307
Homes and businesses with minor damage.

800,000
Cubic yards of debris removed from the city.

39,172
Meals served by the American Red Cross mobile feeding stations during May 2007.

57,786
Hours of work logged by volunteers.

$30.7 million
Amount of low interest loans provided by the U.S. Small Business Administration to residents and businesses in Kiowa County.

$23.1 million
Approved funding so far under FEMA's Public Assistance program.

— Source: *National Weather Service and the Federal Emergency Management Agency*

Kwik Shop/Dillons   *Photo by Bruce Foster*

submitted by: CHRIS CASEY
REPORTER AT THE GREELEY COLORADO TRIBUNE

Greesnburg Residents Bring Back Town

A monument listing the names of the 10 Greensburg residents who died stands in a vacant lot in the middle of the small Kansas town that is rebuilding.

"This town is crazy .... Baby you're lost. Baby you're lost. Baby you're a lost cause."

— Beck

GREENSBURG, Kan. — It looks like a town completely out of place, as if plopped from an alien world onto the prairie. Clinging-to-life trees, crumbled buildings and cartwheeling sagebrush whisper gently against the ever-raging Kansas wind: We're what's left.

Somehow, though, the town remains where it's always stood. It suffered the disastrous fate of sitting directly in the path of one of the nastiest twisters ever spawned by Tornado Alley. The 1.7-mile-wide EF5 — beastliest of tornados — plowed the town on May 4, 2007, as Greensburg residents were getting ready to hop into bed for the night.

Thankfully, most of them were still up at 9:50 p.m. when the monster roared in from the southwest. TV warnings grew more stern and sirens' wails more intense as that fateful evening unleashed a fury that forever changed lives.

Miraculously, only 10 of Greensburg's 1,700 residents died in the storm. It touched off three more EF5s that narrowly missed towns to the north but claimed one more life.

In Greensburg, about all that remained was the courthouse and the 100-plus-foot grain elevator. Townsfolk talk about the bizarre black marks left atop the alabaster tower. They are tire tracks, from a car or truck that left a last earthly imprint before getting tossed heavenward.

The devastation puts Greensburg square into Third World realm. Only a tiny Kwik Stop serves groceries and gas to the remaining inhabitants.

Most remarkable a year after the storm is the collective will of Greensburg residents. Their tenacity stands as tall as those improbable tire tracks in the sky.

Houses are being rebuilt. A new Methodist church is going up. A new water tower stands ready to irrigate a transformation that's perhaps no less daunting than what early settlers faced when they came to scratch out a living in this harsh landscape.

To commemorate how far the town has come and where it's going — it's rebuilding with eco-friendly "green" building materials — President Bush flew in for the Greensburg High School Class of 2008 graduation on May 4, the one-year anniversary of the Big One.

I was there, getting my first glimpse of the town in which my coworker's father and his family were raised. Greensburg buzzed with barbecues, dedications, a dance and a vigil for those who perished.

Despite the desolation, the town rolled out a first-class welcome for the President. Patriot Guard cyclists from across Kansas and beyond lined both sides of Main Street for several blocks. They held hundreds of flapping American flags, creating a spectacle of patriotism as the President whisked by. His motorcade streamed to the graduation site — a temporary gymnasium surrounded by trailers of the defacto high school.

Bush told the graduates, "At this ceremony, we celebrate your year-long journey from tragedy to triumph. We celebrate the resurgence of a town that stood tall when its buildings and homes were laid low. We celebrate the power of faith and the love of family, and the bonds of friendship that guided you through the disaster. Finally, we celebrate the resilience of 18 seniors who grew closer together when the world around them blew apart."

Indeed, perhaps most promising about Greensburg's future is the fact that not one senior in the Class of 2008 left town after the tornado. The disaster forged an uncommon bond and a determination to stick with the people who got you this far.

The president of the senior class said, "Although some people definitely don't consider it a blessing that the tornado hit, there are many good things that came out of it. The strength and unity that has grown, not only in our class, but in the whole town is just great."

Greensburg's spirited graduation, covered by the national media, symbolized what else remains: Defiance, wisdom and pride.

Even the trees are coming back, sprouting crazy shoots of green from trunks and mangled limbs. A tree along Main Street hangs on, its bark shorn away, a piece of twisted and rusted metal drilled deep into its trunk.

My co-worker showed me pictures of the town's drugstore soda fountain in its pre-tornado glory. It looked transported out of "Mayberry RFD" — checkered tile floor, shiny-red topped bar stools, and massive wood counter studded by a gleaming soda stand.

It's long gone, perhaps blown off to Oz. Fortunately, Richard Huckriede, renowned as being the world's oldest soda jerk, survived.

I can't imagine the shock felt by old-timers who in an instant saw the town in which they created so many memories and forged their identity, such as legendary soda jerk, get wiped out. Their mind's eye — like that of my co-worker — still pictures the farmhouses, churches, markets and diners that made Greensburg a distinctive dot on the prairie.

The heart of the town spilled out at the candlelight vigil. Soft glows of flame illuminated hugs and tears under a star-splotched blanket of night. Compassion and warmth — the unyielding human qualities of a tiny prairie burg — beat back against the vast Great Plains darkness.

This town, left in crazy disarray from Mother Nature's wrath, is rebuilding and coming back strong.

Greensburg is anything but a lost cause.

submitted by: NORMAN AND MARCIA UNRUH

216 E. GARFIELD • GREENSBURG, KS 67054

Who Would Have Thought

On May 4th of 2007, I had taken off on that Friday morning to get ready to leave that afternoon. My brother, Steve, and his wife, Jeanne, were getting ready to have the annual Spring Fling at there house in Independence, Ks. While we were there, we were going on Saturday to Marcia's brother-in-law wedding at Coffeyville.

We left Greensburg at 2:30 that afternoon and we had commented that it was awfully hot and sticky. When we got headed east, you could really tell that the atmosphere was hazy all around and it seemed that way till we got to a gas station just north of Independence.

We arrived at Steve and Jeanne's about 8:30 and got the trailer where it needed to be. Marcia, Esther and I finished unhooking the trailer and got everything set up.

We got a chance to visit with Beth and Micah and his son Caleb a little bit. It was getting time to eat supper and Steve's had fixed supper so the kids ate supper out on the picnic table and Marcia, Esther and I ate supper in the camper. After supper, we sat out on the picnic table with the others and were visiting; by then it was dark.

We were laughing and having a good time until Jeanne gets this call from her mother in Wichita and said it looked like a tornado might be headed towards Haviland. It wasn't very long until her mom called back and said it had already hit Paul and Shirley Unruh's house. Marcia said it was going to hit Greensburg. I don't know how she knew but in a few minutes Jeanne's mom had called back and said Greensburg had taken a direct hit. Marcia was on the phone with one of her friends and fellow co-workers from Pratt who had a son-in-law on the sheriff's department there. She would give her blow by blow updates from him.

Marcia immediately wanted to go home and I said not tonight. We needed to try and get some rest and I did not want to pull our trailer down Steve's narrow driveway at night. It was hard to get any rest for not knowing how Chris was or if he even made it through the tornado. With no cell phone connection, we were out of luck.

Marcia needless to say didn't sleep very well. I had just started to relax a little bit when her cell phone rang at 20 minutes till 3 in the morning. It was Chris telling us that he was alright and that he was in Haviland. Lynn Godfrey was working on closing the store down and Chris was cleaning the floor. The siren was blowing when they both went to the meat cooler because that was their designated storm shelter. Chris said the roof of the cooler went up and down and the doors they were holding onto were going in and out and they didn't know how long they could hold on.

The next morning at Independence we got up and ate some breakfast and tried to watch as much of the news as we could. After breakfast, Marcia called her brother-in-law and told him we wouldn't be able to come to his wedding and he understood and they both shed a few tears.

I know that miracles do happen. When I backed under the fifth wheel and got hooked up, we went around to take out the wheel chock. We didn't put it in between the wheels. The reason I know it was a miracle is because we never unhook the trailer from the pickup without putting in the wheel chock first.

Coming across Kansas and not knowing what to expect was very hard. It was the longest 6 ½ hour drive we have had in a long time. Not knowing if Chris had clothing, we had to stop and get him some things to wear. We had a few things along with us, so we were ok.

As we got closer to Greensburg, we knew that we could only get as far as Haviland. That was ok as we just wanted to get to Chris. We were so glad to see him and he was to see us. We pulled the camper back to Denise's house in Pratt and stayed with her for a couple of days to just let everything sink in. We were homeless. That is an awful feeling, and then having to depend on others is not easy. None of us, in this small town, are ones to sit around and ask for help with our hands out. However, we had to, but we were thankful. After two days, we decided that we needed to move to a new location. We decided to move to the Pratt County Lake and sat again vulnerable to the weather for 4 ½ months. There were many nights during that period that we headed to Denise's house to the basement in the middle of the night, only hoping that we'd return the next morning to our belongings.

Norm drove those 30 miles everyday to work. He was getting weary from that routine. We knew we needed a place before the snow began to fly. After all, living in a fifth wheel is not warm during the winter. So, we left our temporary home in Pratt and moved to FEMAVILLE, which looked wonderful to us; much more room and we were warm. We at least had a roof over our heads in Greensburg. It would be easier for Norm to go to work.

It was very frustrating for Marcia as she was not able to find a job. While we were at Pratt, the company she worked for called her and wanted to know if she would go to one of the sister units in Fredonia. She had told the company that she'd be glad to go. Shortly after they had asked her, is when the terrible flood happened there. Marcia went to work in Kinsley to open the Life Care Unit. In September, they had their first and only patient and waited for more to come while scrambling through paper work. Then they had to wait for the rest of the paper work to happen. Marcia worked every day at Medicalodge along beside Julie Miller the Activity Director. Then, the time came that they needed to start getting the unit ready for the BIG opening. It opened January 1 and she is still working there.

On one of those weekends that we both had off, we were working in the yard. Marcia decided to clean out the trash hopper that we purchased from the city. In the bottom of it was a loose straw. She thought she would pick it up and put it in a trash bag. To her surprise, when she did was the glass straw that she thought she lost that belonged to her mom and dad, and was in with the rest of the antique items that were lost on the north wall of her kitchen.

One of the few special items that made it through the storm was an angel that we had given to Marcia's mom when she was in the hospital. She now stands proud among our new items and brings us joy and delight when we see it.

It's been six months since we have been in our home. We are glad that we have it. We love our new home, but it just isn't home.

Through this horrifying ordeal we all learned to be more appreciative of what we have and learn to appreciate all the people that gave of their time to help us.

Thank You Everyone!

submitted by: TIM AND DEANN GARRETT
OLD ADDRESS: 623 S. GROVE • GREENSBURG, KS 67054
NEW ADDRESS: 310 W. ELM • MINNEOLA, KS 67865

Opportunities to Lift Others Up

After the tornado destroyed Greensburg and our home, we temporarily moved to Minneola and I started driving everyday back to Greensburg to deal with all the issues that were involved in trying to get our life back to normal. Each day I would pray that God would give me an opportunity to encourage someone in Greensburg. Little did I know that God was about to give me the ministry opportunity of a lifetime.

President George W. Bush toured Greensburg to survey the damage and offer encouragement to residents of Greensburg. Members of the Kiowa County Ministerial Alliance, of which I was a part, met President Bush in front of the Methodist Church.

Security was tight the day President Bush came. I saw the president's motorcade at the Methodist church, where the alliance was meeting. Another member of the alliance helped me get past a

Ministers with President George W. Bush

Photo by Tim Garrett

security guard so I could join the group of pastors. An official asked who wanted to meet President Bush, and I stepped forward. I was waved down with a security wand and ushered to the area where the president was. Marvin George, who leads the alliance, introduced me. 'This is Tim Garrett, Sir, and he's a missionary with … uh … ' He couldn't remember the name, so I said, "It's Greater Europe Mission, Mr.President.'"

As President Bush got ready to leave, I asked if I could pray for him or if he would pray for us. I said that I knew there was a lot of media around today and that I didn't want to get him in trouble. He smiled and said, "You won't get me in trouble. Don't pray for me, just pray for the people of Greensburg." The president didn't object to joining hands with the pastors while the reporters standing close by. I prayed for the people of Greensburg and then I decided to pray for the president, his two daughters and Laura anyway. When I finished, President Bush said to the group, 'Didn't I tell him not to pray for me? Didn't I make it clear that he was to only pray for the people of Greensburg?" One of the ministers then said, "You should have the Secret Service take Tim out," at which time everyone laughed. The president then said, "This is the first time in seven years that someone has specifically disobeyed an order that I have given. Then he looked directly at me, stepped forward, put a hand on each side of my head, pulled my head down and kissed me on top of my head.

I learned a few months later that a friend of ours from Minnesota had a best friend whose son was killed in Iraq so the president wanted to meet with her friend in his office to give his condolences. As she was waiting in the Oval Office for President Bush to come, she saw the picture of me praying for Greensburg and the president on or by his desk. She then called my friend from Minnesota and said, "Didn't you have a friend from Greensburg that prayed for the president? I saw his picture in the Oval Office."

In the midst of this disaster, I was able to pray for the President of the USA. It goes to show you that there are a lot of opportunities to lift others up if we just take the time to look for them.

submitted by: **SUE GREENLEAF**
R.R. 1 • GREENSBURG, KS 67054

Service to Others

"Tornado alley will live up to its name today," remarked Al Roker on the TODAY show weather report. The statement was alarming enough to lure me from the bathroom where I was putting on my makeup to see just exactly where tornado alley was. Yep, that's us. The tornado symbol was directly on Greensburg. I really didn't give it too much more thought, as I had a busy day ahead. I was leaving with the Greensburg High School Forensics team; headed for Salina to the state forensic tournament.

The weather wasn't mentioned again until about 9:00 p.m. that night as some of us in the motel room were watching TV. They had interrupted regular broadcasting to show the radar and it looked as though a pretty serious storm was heading directly for Greensburg. The weatherman began to say things like, Greensburg is in the direct path of the tornado. It looks like a big one. Reports are coming in, Greensburg took a direct hit. Cell phones continued ringing throughout the 2nd floor of the motel where most of the rooms were filled with Greensburg Forensic students and sponsors. The report came in that the Kwik Shop had been hit. I remembered thinking, that could be bad. A lot of kids could have been there. First report was that 15% of the town was hit, next report 60% and then finally it was reported the water tower was down and 95% of Greensburg was destroyed.

One by one, the 28 students we had in Salina began getting word from friends and family at home. "Our house is gone but my family is alright" became cause for celebration as 28 teenagers grew up quite a bit before our eyes that night. Students, who a few hours earlier were bickering over which movie to see and which restaurant to eat at, were caring for each other and demonstrating maturity beyond their years. It was a long night as we waited to hear from each student's family. Not all the news was good. Kasha Charlton got the word that both her mom and stepdad had been taken to Dodge City to the hospital as a result of injuries they had received. Slowly, but steadily the realization began to soak in that our lives were somehow changed forever.

It has now been 18 months since the tornado. Someone asked me what I had learned since May 4, 2007. I learned that day that something greater than myself was in charge. I have always known that, but experiences like the EF-5 tornado of May 4, bring that message to heart and mind. I got that message again when Jim died so unexpectedly on March 3, 2008. So hopefully, what can be learned from storms that life deals us, is the importance of relationships in this world; the importance of the people around us. Remembering the reaction on a grandchild's face when she felt, heard, and saw the snow crunching under her boots the first time she witnessed snow on the ground. The reaction of a granddaughter feeling thick, green grass between her toes for the first time on a warm spring day. Witnessing a grandbaby react with enthusiasm to the sound of her father's voice as he comes in a room and the joy felt when a grandson runs toward you with outspread arms after spotting you on a small town street. The importance of the little things; because they are the big things.

Our community continues to be blessed with the generosity of our fellowman. Hopefully, we have all learned from this generosity and never pass up an opportunity to be of service to others.

submitted by: DIANNE MURRAY
OLD ADDRESS: 504 S. CHERRY • GREENSBURG, KS 67054
NEW ADDRESS: R.R. 1 • GREENSBURG, KS 67054

I Wanted to Come Back

In May, I was working in Pratt and staying with my son, Levi, who had a house there. We worked that day and came home around 6:00 p.m. The clouds did not look that bad. I could see them in the west but did not pay much attention to them. Levi turned on the TV at around ten to get the news and came and told me that a tornado was going down main-street of Greensburg. A classmate of his, Danny Lehman, was at the house and his Mom also lived in Greensburg.

We all left Pratt and headed to Greensburg. At Haviland, they told us that the road was closed so we went over to the old Cannonball road and continued to town. The road was so muddy and sloppy from the rain that it took 30 minutes to drive the 10 miles. I told Levi to help me watch for any debris in the road because I knew that the tornado had crossed the road somewhere north of town. When we got to the cemetery, we tried to come down that road but a big tree was blocking it. We turned around and went to Main Street. It was blocked by debris lying on the road. We tried to get to Bay street but there was a mound of trees at least 6 foot tall and a block long littering the east and west road. We went back to the Centerview blacktop and went south thinking we could get into town from there. We were trying to get to south Main to check on my Mom. We went south two miles and tried to come across that road but a big tree was lying in the road about a mile and a half from town. We met three other vehicles turning around at the tree that were also trying to get into town. We went back to the highway and tried to get in on the highway from the east and were stopped at the city limits. We went through the truck wash parking lot and went around the swimming pool and went south on Olive street. We drove down this street until we could not go anymore then we would go back and try a different street. We got to the street a block east of the high school and could not go any more so we parked and got out and walked to Mom's house which was still ten blocks away. On the way, we encountered an ambulance and a group of people trying to get a lady out on a stretcher but could not roll it for all the junk. Levi ran over and helped them carry the stretcher to the ambulance. We ran into Tammy Jantz and she told us that Mom and Ron were fine in her cave and that she had taken her a blanket so we could calm down.

We saw a lot of people walking down the street but could not tell who they were. Everyone looked so different. It was a real eerie feeling walking down the streets and we could not tell where we were. We finally got to Mom and told her we were there but it was too far for her to walk so we would be back as soon as we could. The whole upstairs was gone and part of the downstairs was gone on her house. When we got back to the pickup, they had started clearing the streets. It took about an hour before we managed to get to her. As we pulled up, there were some firemen there helping her out of the cave.

Ron had gone on to check on some friends and he helped Norm and Bev Volz out of their house. We got Mom in the pickup and went back south to try to get to my house to see what damage there was. On my house, the roof was gone and part of the walls. We went inside and got the grandfather clock off of the wall where it was still hanging. We went down a half of block and checked on my Aunt Geneva and Cousin Nathan. They were out in the yard and part of her roof was gone also. My roof was 4 X 4 timbers that were double tongue and grooved and a large section of that ended up in her yard a half a block away. We drove around awhile still looking for Ron but could not find him. We went down to the old Dillon's store to find him but he was not there. I found out later that he had went home with Joel and spent the night there. We got to Pratt about four a.m. and slept till 6 a.m.

We went back to access the damage in the daytime. It was worse than what I had ever thought it would be. We went to Mom's house and looked around and her whole upstairs and everything in it was no where to be found. It was just gone. The south wall and the east wall of her house was also blown down. On my house, the living room wall on the west came in, so the living room was full of cinder blocks. The dinning room and a bedroom wall on the east fell out so the yard was full of cinder blocks. Pretty much everything was still in my house but then after all the rain most of it was ruined. We did salvage the photo albums, Mom's quilts and a lot of sentimental things.

In the months that followed, it was so strange to drive around the town that I had grown up in and get lost. The school and the hospital seemed so close because there was nothing in between. There were a lot of times I could not figure out where I was for a bit. We moved what we could from Mom's house and my house into Levi's basement, his yard and a storage unit in Pratt. We all lived with him until June when I bought a house in Pratt for Mom and Ron.

I continued to live with Levi and we worked in Hereford, TX. We were employed to build another ethanol plant but the commute was too long and we could not get home enough to get anything done to clean up the debris. So in September, we came home to cleanup the lots. It was so hard to be so far away and know things needed to be done and not being able to do it. We would come over and clean on the lot and then take a break and drive around. One day, we were driving through the country and drove by an empty farm house owned by Bob and Ruth Ann Wedel with a realtor sign in the yard. We looked at it and decided that I wanted to come back because this is where my heart was. So in November, we moved back to Greensburg and live two miles east and six south of Greensburg. I didn't know how good it would feel to finally be settled in my own house again and to know that I did not have to move.

submitted by: **SUE GREENLEAF**
R.R. 1, • GREENSBURG, KS 67054

Thanks Kansas!

(This was spoken at the Kansas State Fair in Hutchinson in September, 2007 at the opening ceremony).

Is there anyone here from Greensburg?

The F-5 tornado that hit Greensburg, Kansas on May 4th changed the lives of every member of our community. A tornado of that magnitude had not been witnessed for decades. The devastation was widespread and overwhelming. It is however not the most powerful and overwhelming force experienced by the members of the Greensburg community. The outpouring of support, strength, compassion, caring, concern, acts of kindness, thoughts and prayers demonstrated by the citizens of Kansas and people throughout the nation has had an unprecedented impact.

Emergency crews from all over the state were in Greensburg within minutes of the storm. Schools in Haviland and Mullinville were transformed into shelters. Churches became locations to pick up basic essentials such as clothing, diapers and formula. The American Red Cross and Salvation Army were there before daylight. Within days, funds came pouring into Greensburg; from school children selling cookies and lemonade to pennies and change drives from street corners to classrooms. Civic organizations and individuals sent water, storage containers, shovels and gloves. For the days, weeks, and months to follow groups of adults and children could be seen on the lots and streets in Greensburg helping clean up debris, serving water and snacks to workers, and providing meals to the citizens and other volunteers helping in the recovery and cleanup. The efforts of Kansans throughout the state remain a source of constant strength for all of us as we continue the task of bringing our community back stronger than before.

So please join us this evening, giving yourselves a standing ovation, applause and cheers as Greensburg says, THANKS, KANSAS!!!!!

submitted by: **TISH SMITH**
804 W. GRANT • GREENSBURG, KS 67054

Wet, Scared and Worried

For some reason, I was scheduled to work the evening shift the night of the tornado. I normally work the day shift. It had been a quiet evening. My husband, Dennis, had brought me a piece of baseball sized hail that he had picked up on the way home from the track meet in Bucklin. We were glad it didn't hail here- we didn't want our cars hit. Dennis took the trophy hail home and put it in the freezer for our son, Levi, to see when he got home from the Forensics meet in Salina. Of course, Levi never saw it and Dennis's big piece of hail lost its grandeur later that night as it slowly melted away along with everything else in the freezer. Naturally, our vehicles sustained more than a little hail damage that night as big tree limbs tried to flatten them in the hospital parking lot.

The nursing staff had followed hospital protocol and all the patients were sheltered safely in the north basement. Including the Behavior Unit, there were about twenty patients in all. (Actually, about seven of the twenty weren't really patients per-se, they were people who lived at the hospital in the swing bed unit.) We had lined the patients up along the wall in the conference room in their chairs or wheel chairs and two of the patients were taken downstairs in their beds and just rested in them until they were rescued. Not many injured came to the hospital. Most went to the triage center that had been set up by emergency management personnel at the Dillon's store parking lot. We did have an elderly lady who had fallen and cut her head, a young man who had hurt his hip, and several people who complained of back pain. Several people brought their dogs with them. Most just sat and waited for rescue. There wasn't much we could do for them in the basement other than offer them blankets because they were wet and cold. My sister, Relena, who had came there for shelter before the tornado helped the lady who had cut her head and Dennis carried the young man with the hip injury down to the basement and laid him on a "bed" from the physical therapy room. I had called our back up nurse, Malena, when the sirens blew and she was there helping with those injured also. I hesitate to name names because so many people did so much and I'm sure they will never get recognized for what they did, on this side of heaven. I found out after the tornado that several people came to the hospital to help but were told to go to the triage area instead.

When our provider on call, Chris, came to the hospital it was a big relief. I saw him and said, "Thank God you're here!" I needed help calming a man from the outside and knew Chris could take care of the situation. I didn't realize that Chris's house had been demolished by the tornado and he told me weeks later that when I told him I was glad he was there he was thinking, "I'm glad to be here!" I'm sure he had come to the hospital for shelter after going through such a traumatic experience but his rest would not come until hours later.

I must have walked up and down the basement hallway over a hundred times that night. People came and went looking for loved ones. The conference room and the hallway got congested and the bathroom toilets filled up quickly. One of the dogs did his "job" on the floor in the hall and I had the joy of getting that out of the walkway before someone stepped on it. Two of the BHU patients decided they had been there long enough and they had to be convinced to stay. People were wet and scared and worried. One boy asked if I'd seen his grandmother. I told him, "No, I haven't seen her." I'll never forget what happened next. The boy looked at me and said, "Are you ok?" I was taken aback by this young boy's concern. That grandmother was one blessed lady to have such a caring grandson. I later learned the grandmother was one of the tornadoes tragic victims who hadn't made it to safety that night.

When the rescue people came to remove people from the hospital, it was so wonderful! They had come earlier and checked on us all and said they would return. I was so hapy to see them! A lot of people from the community had come to the hospital for shelter and they also helped us control some of the BHU patients who wanted to leave. The BHU nurses had gone to their unit upstairs and grabbed mattresses and put on the floor for patients to lie down on (which was a wonderful idea)! People were everywhere, but for the most part everything went pretty smooth considering what had just happened outside! Some of our patients just couldn't grasp the idea that a tornado had destroyed their room upstairs, but maybe that was a good thing.

Around four a.m., I was put on an ambulance with a patient and my 87 year old mother (who had come to the hospital along with the rest of my family when the sirens blew). Chris had told me he wanted a nurse to go with all of the patients to wherever they were going. I thought everyone was being transferred to the same place but some went to Pratt, some Kinsley, some Bucklin and some Coldwater. I believe all the BHU patients went to Hutchinson and their nurses went with them. Actually, I thought we were all going to Hutchinson. Our ambulance took us to Coldwater. When I realized I was at Coldwater Hospital with my 87 year old mother with no way out, no clothes, no medications for her, no cell phone, I called my oldest son, Joe, and told him I was there and didn't know what to do and I cried on the phone. Joe had come to Greensburg that night and helped rescue people and was already on his way home to Wichita when I called him. He had made it as far as Pratt but turned around and drove to Coldwater and rescued my mother and I and brought us to Greensburg. By then it was six o'clock in the morning and Dennis was walking down the road because Greensburg was being evacuated and they had told him to leave. So Joe picked him up and we went to our home (we were some of the few fortunate that still had a home) and packed our bags and went to Wichita with Joe and watched on TV as news unfolded about the EF-5 tornado that made Greensburg history.

submitted: KATHY SENST
14 S. CEDAR • GREENSBURG, KS 67054

That Night is a Blur

Where do you start? It has been a long year and half. Our family really enjoyed reading Janice's book and thus decided to write a second part to our story.

We ordered a house from Wardcraft back in July of 2007. We were able to save our basement foundation but did add on a foot so the basement ceilings could be higher. We moved the stairway to open up the main part of the house. Added a master bathroom and made most everything handicap accessible. The single car garage was turned into a sewing room and brought the laundry room upstairs. Dick and I went to Clay Center after deciding to go with them and in one day we made all of the major decisions concerning outlets, cabinets, color of wood trim, sinks, windows, doors, siding, etc. It was one long day.

Considering never doing (and not planning on doing it again!) the part of picking out everything and doing it all in one day, I'm very happy with our home. Yes, there are a few things that I would change if I did it over again, but nothing that I can't live with.

We went up once while the house was being built to see if there was anything to be changed. Aaron was working for Wardcraft at the time. It is neat that he was able to help build our home. He also helped deliver it and put it on the foundation. The house was delivered the end of November. Then the troubles began. Our salesman that originally took our order resigned so we were put with another salesman. Things just did not go smooth after that. By begging for days, they finally came and put in the stairway so that we could get the furnace in and get heat going in the house. They did not come back to finish the house until the middle of January. We must have had the slowest finishers in the world. They did not finish up until the middle of March. I then painted several of the rooms and ended up painting everything as I was not happy with the paint job at all. Now was the time to do it before the flooring was put down. We then had the floor coverings put in. So finally on March 29th, we moved into our new home.

We may have moved in but things sure are not done yet. We are learning to be electricians and carpenters. The basement at this time has studs, most wiring and the bathroom fixtures. Hopefully the sheetrock can be done soon and then move into the basement.

The boys and a couple of friends started our deck when we were on vacation this summer. It was so nice to come home to half a deck. Hopefully within the next month we can get that finished.

The yard work is coming along. We have hauled in a lot of dirt. So we have moved, watered, moved some dirt and watered some more. We have seeded the front yard and plan to do the backyard in the spring.

There are still things to do but hopefully some day the list will be finished and we can truly enjoy our home. It has been a long ordeal and we wouldn't wish it on anyone. But with the prayers and wishes from everyone we have been able to make it through without too many obstacles. I never dreamed that when I would walk up those stairs that night I would find what I did. By listening to the fire pager I realized that it had hit pretty much the whole town but still it was hard to fathom until you see it in the daylight. That night is a blur to me and that is good.

The stories that have come from that night are amazing. I do believe that God's hand was over this town and protected many of us. We have learned that material things are nothing compared to lives.

I want to thank Janice for putting this book together. We talked about how a book would be a good idea to hear how everyone survived the storm. There were stories that I read in the first book that I had not heard about so by someone recording these stories we will be able to pass on this small part of history to our families.

First Baptist Church   *Photo by Bruce Foster*

submitted by: ESTHER UNRUH
216 E. GARFIELD • GREENSBURG, KS 67054

Thanks to Everyone That Helped

The Monday following the tornado was a morning I will never forget. I was scared and yet, I was anxious not knowing how bad my town was hit, and how many of our friends were still around.

The wait was two hours to get back into town. We walked and talked to a lot of our friends and neighbors while we were waiting. We were delayed due to the anhydrous ammonia leak they had found.

We had family that came from Wichita to help us salvage our belongings. They couldn't believe their eyes. Everywhere you turned it was all the same; what belonged to whom.

When we got to the check point, they wrote down all the addresses of where you could go and only could go there.

We first went to my brother Chris's apartment to see what we could get from there. His roof had just separated and you could see through it. We managed to save lots of things. It was hard to get everything because of the insulation all over everything. We finished there and then went to our house. The emotions we all had were awful.

The new kitchen that had just got finished was gone, the roof was gone, and my Bible that my grandparents gave me for my graduation was gone. Before we could get into the house, we had to have two large oil tanks moved. They were in front of the window that we had to climb through. The guys, from KDOT that Dad works with, helped us get them pulled back.

We were fortunate enough that we had our 5th wheel camper with us the night of the tornado. We lived in it at the Pratt County Lake for 4½ months. At least, it was home.

My job at Duckwall's in Greensburg was gone. It was so sad as I made a lot of friends. After the tornado, I transferred to the Alco store in Pratt. That was hard as it was so big and different, but everyone was so kind and helpful to help me learn their system. After mom started to work in Kinsley, at the Life Care Center formally the BHU at Greensburg, we couldn't afford for mom to drive me to Pratt and then drive to Kinsley, so I transferred to the store in Kinsley.

We were able to put our home back on the same location that we were in before the tornado, except we moved it to the east a little.

I just am so thankful that we were all ok, and that my brother made it through the tornado.

Thanks to everyone who helped us.

submitted by: ERICA FOSTER AND KAYLEE PITTS
OLD ARRESS: 122 W. GRANT • GREENSBURG, KS 67054
NEW ADDRESS: 10408 W. RIVER RD. • PRATT, KS 67124

Prayed and Prayed

We were sitting in the living room, and my sister and her husband called and said they were coming over because we were in a tornado watch. They came over, and we chatted with each other for a while, and then my brother-in-law Brandon says, "The tornado siren should go off any minute!" That second it went off, as if on cue. So, we all headed to the basement. Of course, the men wanted to see the tornado, so they kept going out the back door. We didn't know exactly how serious the situation was. Alyssa was screaming at them telling them to get in the basement. Then, we could hear the message machine upstairs where mom's best friend was screaming, "Sandy get in the basement there's a huge tornado headed straight for Greensburg!!!" One of the men went up and got the phone and brought it down. The phone rang again, and it was mom's friends daughter screaming in panic that the tornado was headed for us. So at that point we went into the little room in the back of the basement, because dad always said that would be the strongest part of the basement. He had been trying to get mom to let him put a safe room in the basement for about six months, but she said she would never get in it because she's claustrophobic. He had been saying, if there's ever a tornado, that basement's going to cave in on us. It's not going to hold. So we all had that thought going through our heads. So, mom, Alyssa, me, Kaylee, and Alyssa's baby, Jason, all headed to that back room. Dad stayed in the other room because he said, if the tornado actually hits, he was going to be out there so he could make a path to the door. He fully expected the basement to cave.

We then discovered that we did not bring a flashlight down there with us, so we were debating who would go upstairs and get the flashlight. I found the candles from my wedding in the basement, and I lit those so no one would go upstairs. Brandon then came in the little room with us, and we took pictures of each other with the camera he had brought downstairs and sang happy birthday over and over again to keep my daughter calm. Then, the lights and the tornado siren suddenly went off. We sat there with the candles knowing that we were in trouble. I was sitting by the coal chute, and then I started to hear the tornado. It was an extremely loud roar, and I started hearing debris hitting the house. I looked at mom in panic and said, "Do you hear that?" She freaked out and stood up and said, "NO, NO! It's ok!" I said, "I'm blowing these candles out!" and did. We were in the pitch dark.

Then the air pressure changed. My ears started popping over and over again, and then I could hear the house literally breaking apart above us. The windows blew out like an explosion had gone off. Boards were breaking. Then, the entire house lifted off of it's foundation, and we could feel air above us. I kept looking up trying to see what was going on, and debris just kept getting dumped in my face. The house slammed down on top of us leaving just enough room not to totally crush us. The pipes that had run along the ceiling landed on top of Alyssa, Brandon, and mom, hurting them but not severely. They started screaming that they were hit, and I was screaming, "God save my baby!" This went on for what seemed like hours, but was actually only a couple of minutes. Alyssa and I then started to panic, because dad was in the other room, and we couldn't hear him. We screamed and screamed for him, and he didn't answer. Finally it all calmed down, and we heard dad's voice. We took a role call to make sure everyone was alive, and then Brandon opened his cell phone, and the light from that showed us what kind of shape we were in. The house was right on top of us so bad that we couldn't even sit up straight. Of course, our first thoughts were that we had to get out of there, and what the heck is keeping this house from coming all the way down on top of us? My dad was over by the door, and saw that the house had moved over the stairs blocking our opening, and asked if someone could get to him to help him find a way out. Brandon barreled out there, and next thing we new dad said Brandon was out.

Water started seeping in behind us, and Kaylee and I were in the very back. More and more water was coming in, and the hot water heater was knocked over spewing hot water on us. We had to crawl over that to get over to where dad was. We finally got there, and the hole was where the stairs had been. Brandon pulled Alyssa and I and the babies out first. When I got out, my breath was taken away, because we got out when the tornado hooked back around and hit the town again. The wind was blowing so hard it was hard to breathe. Alyssa and I quickly figured out that there was no garage, and there was debris everywhere. Our shoes had been ripped off of our feet and we were barefoot. I found my car and told Alyssa to get in it. The windows were blown out, and we were getting pelted by rain and hail, and the car was violently rocking around in the wind. That's when I started praying my little heart out. I looked at what was left of the house next to me, and prayed and prayed. Finally, my dad made it out; barely.

It was obvious that we needed to find shelter because this thing was obviously not over. We made it to the street, and decided to go to the hospital. We were walking in knee deep water with downed power lines everywhere; looking through the lightning and the trees could not have looked more eerie. We made it down the road to the hospital where there were wrecked trucks, and the smell of gasoline. One of the doors on the truck got sucked up into the air, and then would come back down and get sucked up again. It was HUGE and there were a lot of other big things flying around. The hospital was destroyed and there was no way to get into the front door. We went as fast as we could to the side door, and opened it. The ceiling tile fell in as we opened the door, but we could just barely make it down the hallway into the safety of the basement where there was a lot of people. We sat there in the dark with the sirens going off for 2 hours when more and more injured kept coming in. My neighbor came in, and every bone in her face was broken, her neck was broken, and both her arms were broken. (Roberta Schmidt). Since my mom, sister, and brother-in- law were hurt, someone came and got us in a pick up, and took us to the Dillon's parking lot triage area, where we were then shipped in an ambulance to Pratt hospital. They all got x-rays. There were no broken bones, so our family took us to Hutchinson where we stayed in a motel. Two weeks later, my parents bought a house in Pratt, and so here we are.

submitted by: PAT AND DONNA GREENLEAF
OLD ADDRESS: 10463 AVE. 31 • GRENSBURG, KS 67054
NEW ADDRESS: 10350 SW SUNFLOWER DR. • PRATT, KS 67124

We Are Survivors

The night of the tornado I had been working at the hospital and left approximately at 9:00 p.m. Driving home, I never thought the weather seemed too severe. There was a tornado watch on the TV. I had asked the nurse if she wanted me to stay. Neither one of us seemed to think anyone was in any eminent danger, so I went on home. You always hear of these types of disasters, but you never live them. We had had tornado warnings for the last two to three weeks.

Of course, we thought that it was just another warning until we heard on the TV that there was a wall tornado coming straight for Greensburg and for everyone to take shelter.

One of our son's was coming from Kansas City that night and called us as he was going through Pratt at about 9:30 p.m. (Approximately 30 miles away). His dad told him we were headed for the basement and that if he had not heard from us in fifteen minutes, not to come on. We thank God that for once in his life he listened to his father.

We went to the basement with our cell phones, cordless phone and a flash light and turned on the TV; knowing that we'd be going back upstairs in a few minutes. The TV went out about 9:40 p.m. We started to hear the hail breaking the windows, and then we heard a noise like an airplane engine starting, at that point Pat said we needed to get up off the couch and to start to go over to the game table next to the staircase, as we reached the table, we set our phones and flashlight down on the table and our whole upstairs started coming down on us. We were knocked to the ground and we crawled into a space underneath the staircase that had the hot water heater and furnace. Once we got in there, we were safe, but we were trapped. If we would have stayed on the couch, we probably would have been killed. After about five minutes, we decided to try to make our way out. We found a board from our upstairs ceiling and Pat started to break through the sheet rock in the downstairs bathroom. Then we heard it again. It was coming back over us. So, we stayed there for a while longer; this time in no hurry to escape our safe space. Once, we thought it was done, we continued to break through the bathroom wall and we headed for the staircase and we were again trapped. We waited there for what seemed to be about twenty minutes. Then our neighbor from the north, Stan Robertson, and Roger Staats came calling our names, as well as Gene and Cory West. They dug us out of our basement.

We all started walking towards town picking up our neighbors along the way. We got to the city limits and Roger said, "Let's just walk to my house on Main Street and you can all spend the night there." So, we were headed for Main Street, slowly realizing that not just the houses in our area were gone, but the whole town was gone! Some people from Haviland picked us up and drove us to Main Street. We got to Roger's house to find it sitting catty corner on his lot. We all kind of went our own way at that point. Pat and I decided to go to the hospital to see if we could help there. Once we finally got there, they told us there was no one there and the command center was at Dillon's. At that point, I was devastated; knowing that I had just left there and had no idea whether or not they made it through the storm. So, we walked to Dillon's from the hospital hoping to find someone we knew. When we got to Dillon's, 54 highway was lined with ambulances; taking people out that were injured. They turned the local tavern into a first aid station to treat people with minor injuries and they made the tire shop into the morgue. We stayed in Dillon's for what seemed to be a long time. We had no communication with the outside world. If you still had your cell phone, it did not work. You couldn't talk to anyone to let them know you were okay! I guess we just walked around in a daze until all of a sudden someone came up from behind us and tapped us on the shoulder, and it was our son! Then everything seemed to be okay!

After that, Steve Goering and Bill McMurry found us and took

Greensburg High School

Photo by Stacy Barnes

us to Steve & Debbie's house. We then stayed with Wilder's, until we moved to a fifth- wheel trailer at Linda & Tom Brower's. We stayed there until we could move into a FEMA trailer that is now sitting on our land. We never thought we'd be thankful for living in a FEMA trailer, but we are very grateful!

We feel very blessed that Alton Unruh came by and offered us help from the Mennonite's and they were wonderful to help us in our devastation. We were always the givers and it was hard to be the taker, but we've learned to. The Salvation Army, the Mennonite Disaster Relief organization, and all of the churches were wonderful to all of us, as well as all of the volunteers throughout the whole country. We had no where to eat, sleep, get gas, or money from the bank. We were given shelter, food, water, and clothing. We want all of you to know we were not victims, we are survivors. The reason that we are survivors is because of the many donations and prayers that people from all over the world gave to us. Whether it was a monetary donation, clothing, furniture, bedding or a prayer, we want you to know that's what sustained us through this tragedy. May life bring you a reflection of the kindness you've shown to us. It's a comfort to know we can count on each other through whatever life brings. Thank you from the bottom of our hearts! This tornado was a category EF-5 and destroyed 95% of what used to be Greensburg. Fortunately, as a Christian, no one can take your hope from you and we know that Jesus is the anchor in the storms of life! God Speed!

submitted by: CARMEN RENFROW
620 N. MAIN • GREENSBURG, KS 67054

An Underlying Sadness

On the day of May 4th, I was working at a friends' retail store. The radio was busy with storm warnings all day. A customer came in, someone who was working in town and living at the RV park, and told me that there were several storm chasers stationed on the west side of town. He had spoken with them and they indicated they were expecting a lot of storm activity in this area. They were just waiting for the action to start!

He asked me what he should do if a storm hits here. I told him the motel across the street from him has a basement. I explained the storm siren and what to listen for and told him to run, not walk, for that shelter if it went off.

With the radio reports and now the information that storm chasers were at our door steps, I was getting a little uneasy. I've lived in Kansas for a long time. I've heard storm sirens go off more times than I can count and usually there isn't much to it. The wind blows, it rains, maybe some hail and it's over. Life goes on as usual, no big deal. But this time, something just didn't feel right, as I said, uneasy.

I got off work about 6:00 p.m. and Chance Little came on shift to finish up the night until 9:00 pm. My husband, William, and I barbecued steaks, had a beer, and settled in to watch some TV and watch the weather. It was about 9:15 to 9:30 when the tornado siren went off; one long blast. I hollered to William, "Here it is!" I grabbed my shoes, got them back on, ran for the dogs' leashes (we have 3 dogs), and grabbed the cat. I had one dog on a leash in one hand, the cat under my other arm. William had the other two dogs on their leashes and a flashlight (the electricity always goes out in a storm whether there's a tornado or not). We ran out the back door and headed next door where my sister Glenna and her husband, Marvin, lived. They had a basement. We have a storm shelter that we hadn't yet got the bugs and spider webs and creepy crawlies cleaned out yet and besides, if there's going to be a storm I want to be with family.

My brother-in-law met us at the door, said to come on in and head for the basement if we wanted to. He was going to finish watching his movie. Glenna, William, and I, along with our 3 dogs, our cat and their cat were all in the basement. We had a couple of flash lights with us and sure enough very soon after reaching the basement the power went out. The wind was really howling and soon we heard glass breaking. Glenna was yelling for Marvin to "get down here!" Eventually, he did come down to the basement. The basement windows were flapping back and forth and the sound of the wind was deafening.

After a short while, the wind let up and it was pretty quiet. The men went up stairs to discover glass broken all over the kitchen and water dripping from the ceiling. They told us to stay downstairs for awhile until they could get the glass at least partially cleaned up. William went outside and across the yard to our house. The air was dead calm. He saw that our house was still standing as was our garage. The garage door was ripped off and shreds of it were on the ground and between our vehicles, but none of our vehicles were damaged!

He saw his 18-wheeler, which was parked in the street in front of our house, turned over on its side. The trees in both our yards looked like a bomb had gone off; branches were strewn everywhere. He looked in the garage and about that time the wind picked up again. He started back over to Glenna & Marvin's house and by the time he got to their back door, the wind was so strong he could hardly stand up! Back to the basement!

We were hit a second time, and this time it was much stronger. The whole house shook, more breaking glass, dust sifted down from the basement ceiling. The wind was even louder than before. It seemed to last forever; usually these things last maybe a minute and they're done. But this second hit just kept coming!

Finally, the wind calmed; there was still wind but not as bad. We came up from the basement to utter destruction! Most of the roof was gone, all the windows were blown in, and everything was soaked and covered with … what ? … YUK … from the tornado!

Since our house was still standing, we went there to spend the night. We didn't know the whole town was destroyed! We didn't know people had lost their lives!

The wind was blowing, but not bad. Clouds covered the dark sky and lightning was flashing non-stop all night. We tried to sleep, but it was a fitful night. At dawn we were startled by someone banging on our door and yelling, "You have to evacuate NOW"!

We decided to go to Hutchinson about eighty miles away to Glenna & Marvin's daughters' home. We were able to get our vehicles out. Thankfully, they survived the storm. We drove across the lawn and down to the street. The drive way was blocked by a tangle of tree branches and metal debris about ten feet high. It was just past sunrise as we drove through town … OH, MY GOD! The destruction was un-believable! Our town was gone! Piles of bricks and debris where once stood lovely old buildings. Homes destroyed, completely. The trees were literally stripped of their leaves. We drove through town a short distance towards a friend's house. We wanted to see if she was

OK. An officer stopped us, no one we recognized, and told us we had to leave. By the time we reached the highway and turned to leave town, the tears were falling and didn't stop for several miles.

Eventually, we rented a house in Mullinville, KS, just ten miles west of Greensburg, until our house was repaired. We were able to move back August 18 & 19, 2007. My sister, Glenna and her husband, Marvin, had to have their house bulldozed and their lot leveled. They bought a cute house in Bucklin, KS, about twenty-two miles west of Greensburg and have settled in.

So many friends and acquaintances are scattered about the country in other towns. Some will be back, some won't. No matter how nice Greensburg is built back, no matter how much we grow and prosper; and I hope it happens that way; we will never have our home back. The Greensburg I grew up in will never be the same. So many familiar places are gone forever. The planning goes on for a new and better town and that's good; but, there's always an underlying sadness for those of us whose roots are deep in Greensburg. One friend commented, "I wonder when I can drive down Main Street and not cry?"

submitted by: SCOTT AND SUSAN REINECKE
803 S. SYCAMORE • GREENSBURG, KS 67054

One Awful Night

Life can change … or end in a moment. That is what I learned as the tornado of May 4, 2007, destroyed our home and town.

The evening was a typical Friday night. I was at the grocery store at closing time when one of the sackers came in to tell me my husband, Scott, was in the parking lot waiting for me. He told me there was a big storm coming and wanted to put my car in the body shop to protect it from hail damage. I looked at the sky and my breath was taken away by the massive storm clouds moving our way. The air around me was oddly still. Once home, I put groceries away and changed into comfy clothes. It registered that Scott was running around the house in a very focused mode. He stopped and looked at me and said, "Susan, put jeans on, sturdy shoes and come to the basement." I said "really???" Scott said, "I'm afraid this is going to be bad, I can just tell." Scott got together all the important things he could think of and took them to the basement. The important things to him were computers, Alex's senior pictures, my purse, emergency kit, medicine, wedding pictures, water, and Captain Crunch. When I got to the basement, I went under the stairs and sat in one of the two folding chairs he had set up. "Are these for us?" I asked. "No, Mom and Dad will be over and I want them to have something to sit on." "How do you know they will come over I asked … should I call?" "No, I just know they will." Later, we found out they did not have the TV on and did not know anything was happening until the tornado siren sounded and didn't quit! The doorbell rang and Harry and Jean joined me under the stairs.

Scott was still running around like crazy trying to think of anything we were going to need in an emergency. He just knew this was it, the big one. I am so glad he was aware or I would have still been barefoot! I thought to myself, a tornado won't hit. They never do. We always go outside to watch the clouds when we hear the tornado siren. That's what Kansan's do! But I listened to the TV and scanner with growing dread as this monster tornado headed towards our town. I talked to several friends on my cell phone to make sure they were safe. Our son Alex, enjoying his senior year as a Greensburg Ranger, was with the Forensics group in Salina. Thank God, I don't have to worry about where he is. But where are all his friends? I pray they are safe. Alex called us about ten minutes before the storm hit. He had just heard about a big tornado moving our way and were we all under the stairs safe? "Yes, Alex. We love you and we are all safe. Have fun!" I talked with a friend who was going next door to tell her neighbors to come to her basement as they didn't have one. Then the hail came and we hung up. I really hoped my friend went to her cellar instead of next door. I thought the hail must be huge to be that loud for us to hear all the way in the basement. "I think I'll go see the hail" said Scott's dad, Harry. "No Dad, stay down here." Scott had pulled a mattress from the bedroom downstairs as far into the space under the stairs as he could to give us more protection and block the under stairs opening. There's Buster, our cat, clawing over the mattress to be with us under the stairs. He ran under Jean's chair and didn't make a sound. Then ….

"My ears are popping," I screamed. I thought my head would explode before the pressure gave. And that's when the tornado hit! Noise, I hope to never hear again. I heard no train, but how to describe a house being ripped apart? Huge crashes and bangs and thumps. "Is our house gone Scott??" "No, everything's fine Sweetie." I'm thinking--Why is there water dripping on me?? Maybe a pipe broke. What is that smell? Dust from our homes' day one. And the sweet smell of fresh wood. Trees were ripped up and torn apart. I was terrorized and all I could think as I gripped my mother-in-law's leg in a grip that said if-I-go-you-are-coming-with-me … I don't want to die in a tornado! She tried to comfort me, as well as my husband and father-in-law. They were all very calm but I was upset enough for all of us! Then quiet. Harry starts to go upstairs to see what all happened when I scream, "my ears are popping again." "Get back under here Dad," yells Scott. And another tornado hits, or as we found out later the inflow as it tries to form again.

Our basement stairs held. In fact, we were lucky and had walls and partial roof left. Scott and Harry took an hour to dig a path to the front door and finally came for Jean and I to come upstairs. Jean and I had been sitting in the basement waiting. I reveal an important secret to her,"you and Harry are getting the Booster of the Year Award. You will get your award this Tuesday at the awards banquet." Actually, it would be a year later as we had no idea of the magnitude of the damage. I round the stairs and see the night sky. "Oh My God!" We make our way thru destruction to the front door. I glance around in dazed horror at what used to be our home. I cannot comprehend. Harry is looking for his red pick-up that he had parked in our driveway. He finally sees a bit of red on our front porch underneath the giant pine tree that used to stand at our corner of Morton and Sycamore. Scott tries calling Alex one more time to let him know we are ok and he gets a connection! He is able to tell Alex we are all ok and the neighbor, Rick Engelken, said, "tell Shane we are ok, too." We find out later Alex didn't hear Scott say his grandparents were with us and ok so he worried about them all night.

We start making our way towards the highway. We carefully climb over electrical wires but with no sparks anywhere we hope they are dead. I hear and see a loud piece of equipment which looks to be clearing a street and I ask how could they get here so soon? Time had lost its' meaning. We see a man who asks us where he is at. We look around and can't tell him. There are no houses for landmarks, no street signs. We are lost in our own town. It was a most awful feeling. We walk north on Main Street and a truck comes by with the driver shouting if anyone wants a ride to Dillon's parking lot to hop in. They have come up from Sun City to help. We climb in the back. As we ride down Main Street, I can't believe my eyes. Everything is gone. Our town is gone. The High School, banks, stores … everything destroyed. How many people are dead? There have to be many, many lives lost with this amount of destruction. Were the kids out cruising

Main Street? Please let everyone be ok. I hear a woman crying for help to the east of Main Street. I turn glazed eyes in that direction. I have always wished I would have been able to help her, but I couldn't.

We get to Hwy. 54 and see emergency vehicles, ambulances everywhere. Lights are flashing like a 4th of July from hell. We see many people gathered in the parking lot; some wounded, kids asleep on their mama's shoulders. One girl had a cell phone that still worked so we lined up to use her phone to call loved ones. She stood on a chair and held it up to the sky to stay connected. I called Alex again and as I started to cry he told me, "Mom you need to hold it together because there are people here in Salina that haven't heard from their families and I need to see if you have seen them." I started yelling out names to people and they would answer "yes, I saw them" or "yes, I heard they were ok." Sometimes there was no reply to a name called out and my heart went out to that child wanting news of their loved ones. Buses were parked and loading to take people to emergency shelters in Haviland, Mullinville, and Bucklin; our neighboring towns. They opened up their homes and hearts to us, as all the people who showed up to help in our time of need, and we are forever grateful.

This is the story of one awful night that happened in my life. We have stayed to rebuild our lives in Greensburg. Our businesses were part of the 5% of the town that were spared; Greensburg Collision and Red Shed Antiques. Times had been tough. So just the year before, we had dropped the insurance we carried on the buildings for twenty years. To say we feel blessed to have them still standing is an understatement. Minor note, one of two doors that blew in at the body shop landed on my car but there weren't any hail dents. We were able to have the buildings repaired, new roofs, some walls, and doors. I opened my antique business for a short while. There were big holes in the roof but no danger to customers if they stepped around debris. Everybody that came in wanted to hear my story and they would stand there with tears streaming down their faces and so would I. It didn't take long for me to realize that this was not going to work for me. It was all just stuff and I would be happy to give it all away. It had no meaning to me anymore.

We heard the Fire Department and Ambulance Service were desperate for buildings to house their emergency equipment. With the customer base for the body shop gone (people who moved away and everyone else with new cars), the outlook was grim for auto body work. The fire trucks just barely fit but we made it work. The firemen were so grateful to have a building and a house with beds; an Awesome bunch of guys!

For the past year, we have been working to open our new business; one we have dreamed of, and now have the opportunity. We are excited that "Studio 54" a Stained Glass Studio and Gallery will open soon in the Sunchips Incubator Building.

But, if a tornado happens here again, I'm out of here! Seriously!

submitted by: ELLEN PETERS
R.R. 1, BOX 72 • GREENSBURG, KS 67054

Normal Went Away

On May 1, 2007, my husband's brother, George Peters died in the Hutchinson Hospice House; a very long time after his diagnosis of prostate cancer. His wake was being held in Buhler Kansas on the evening of May 4, 2007 to be followed by the funeral in Medora the following morning. After having attended the wake and having had supper with family members, Abe and I arrived back in Kiowa County about 10:15 p.m. and were stopped from going on home by a line of traffic at the east edge of Haviland. Another motorist, just walking around on the highway told us that high winds had brought some electric lines down. The Highway Patrol was not allowing anyone to proceed west. I turned on the Great Bend radio station and heard the announcer say that there was a report that a tornado had set down possibly, north of Greensburg. I told Abe that I sure hoped our friends who lived up in that area were all right.

It was still very windy. After awhile, Abe and I decided to get out of traffic and go to our farm by a different route instead of waiting for the traffic to clear. When we got home, we too, were without water and electricity and so we just went to bed because we had to get up early the next day to attend the funeral.

Several times during the night, we both woke up and I would say to Abe each time, (knowing by the radio/alarm by our bed that the electricity had not come on yet), that I needed to determine where I was going to get my shower in the morning before we went to the funeral. Finally about 5:30 a.m., he said, that if I just had to have a shower I should just go into town to "Helen's house" and take my shower.

The Helen, to whom he referred, was my very dear friend, Helen Rule. I had been taking a shower at her home every Monday, Wednesday and Friday after my Pilate's class and before work for the last three years. So, I decided to do just that. I grabbed what I needed and headed for town to take a shower at Helen's house.

I got to town about 5:45 a.m. I came in the back way, on the dirt road that goes by the golf course and just east of the Iroquois Center. When I got to the Iroquois Center, I could not believe my eyes. The big sign on the brick wall was broken and on the ground and every window in our fleet of company cars was shattered. Gutters were hanging off the roof and swinging in the breeze and the big red barn across the street was missing.

Unable to comprehend what had gone on, I continued west into town and was horrified at what I saw. The town was unrecognizable. When I got to Main Street, I started weeping and saw six people in fireman suits walking side by side down the street. Every business on Main Street was just a pile of rubble. My first thought was that I was dreaming and I just wanted to wake up.

I continued on to the Highway and found no refuge there. The

Incubator Building   *Photo by Bruce Foster*

stop light was gone and so was Fleener's and everything else that I was expecting to see.

I became very alarmed for Helen at that point, because tough as she always was, she was on continuous oxygen and I knew she would need help. It never dawned on me at that point that the city had long since been evacuated. I tried in vain to find the house to which I had been to so very, very often. I could not find it. It was just impossible to get my bearings. I eventually found my way back toward the Iroquois Center and came upon a man in a pick up with a red light on the top. I stopped him and crying all the while, said, "I know I am probably not supposed to be here but I really, really need to find my friend. She's on oxygen and she cannot do without it very long." He told me to go to KDOT and someone there would tell me where my friend was.

I made my way to KDOT. I told the woman who stopped me there that I was desperately looking for my friend. She asked me what my friend's name was and I told her, Helen Rule. She then said, "She is at the shelter in Haviland." Instead of being grateful, I was immediately angry because I thought, 'this woman does not even know Helen, how does she know where she is' and felt dismissed.

Anyway, with no other options, I went home and told Abe who was all dressed and ready to go the funeral, that Greensburg was gone. "There is nothing left," I told him. He just stared at me as if I was talking a foreign language. I told Abe I could not go to the funeral because I had to find Helen. Also, I am the nurse for the community mental health center and I knew that our adult consumers who were living independently would have probably also lost their homes and would need someone to help them through this crisis.

I left then, for Haviland and found Helen in the shelter just as the lady at KDOT had said. Her son, from Denver had beaten me to her by about ten minutes. She was alive and breathing but looked very dazed. Of course, everyone else did; as I looked around the shelter and saw many of my friends. It did make her smile, however, when I told her that I did not know about the tornado until I tried to come to her home to take a shower.

I don't remember who asked me to help out with the Red Cross but I was privileged to spend the next three days working with them and calling in prescriptions to surrounding pharmacies to replace prescriptions lost in the tornado. In the huge sea of need, it was such a small thing to do but I was so glad that I could do even that little bit.

This tornado experience is an overwhelming experience. I did not lose my personal home and possessions and I will always be very grateful for that. The overwhelming part for me was to see so many of my friends and neighbors in such great distress, to see the indescribable destruction, to witness the quick, efficient and generous response both immediately and long term, to see how very long it takes to recover from a natural disaster of this magnitude, to lose the friends who needed to move away and those who died. I have witnessed disasters on television all my life and always thought, "oh, those poor people" and then went back to my life.

A journalist from Newman University, my alma mater, interviewed me about the tornado for their quarterly magazine several months after the tornado. I told him in that interview, "That May 4, 2007 was the day NORMAL WENT AWAY." Only now do I realize in how many ways, such a disaster changes "normal".

My friend, Helen, died a victim of cancer on November 4, 2008. I will always wonder how much effect the physical, emotional and mental stress of the tornado had to do with how soon she died. I miss her very much.

submitted by: ED AND MARQUITA FROST
OLD ADDRESS: 313 S. BAY • GREENSBURG, KS 67054
NEW ADDRESS: 210 E. ELM • BUCKLIN, KS 67834

Material Things Come And Go

Typical day in the life of Ed. That morning the staff at Iroquois Center had a relaxed social time, it was fun and good memories were shared. Work was quite routine after that. I was joyful that Friday had finally come. I wanted to get home and mow the lawn before the rain made it impossible once again. The rain this year had made mowing your lawn a time management challenge. Competition with neighbors was fun--who would get their lawn mowed first? Today for once I did!

Home has always been my sanctuary. My wife prepared dinner and I watched the news. After dinner we talked about plans for Saturday. My plan for Saturday morning was to go do some prep work on the church parsonage. I dreaded the thought of preparing the parsonage for painting, the siding of the house had been so badly neglected.

Weather report was the familiar talk of possible severe thunderstorms moving in tonight. My wife and I usually enjoy sitting on the front porch and watching the lightning and being cooled by the rain filled breeze. Tonight, we thought that might be an enjoyable thing to do.

Watching some favorite television shows we were updated on the supposedly coming thunderstorms. As the evening progressed, the reports were getting worse. We paid a little closer attention when stated that a severe storm was moving northeast. We talked about family and hoped they were paying attention to the weather too. My mom called me every day and today was no different, we talked about a lot of things and then about what she should do if the tornado sirens went off. She said she would NOT go to the storm shelter she would just stay in her apartment and sit in her bathtub if the sirens went off. Encouragement to go to the storm shelter was futile! We wished each other good-night and hung up. To check on the weather, Marquita and I walked out to the back yard. As we looked southwest, we saw one of the largest tallest clouds we'd ever seen. It was beautiful and awesome and yet sparked fear, it was huge!

My wife seems to live in the kitchen; don't know what all she does in there but I usually just try to stay out of her way and not disturb her. Tonight was an exception--reports of a tornado sighting south of Greensburg prompted me to demand we get ready to head to the basement. The sirens started going off so down we went. Marquita had her purse and the telephone; both usually would have been left upstairs on the counter. I asked why she was bringing them and she said she really didn't know; just felt like she needed to. She said we would call my mom and our daughter and make sure they were all taking precautions.

Generally at home, we go barefoot, or for me just socks; tonight was no different. I didn't think to get shoes or anything. Downstairs, we had a radio, flashlight, candles, matches, and a coffee can. I called family and everyone was taking proper steps; still couldn't get my mom to go to the shelter. This worried us as we had been watching TV and keeping abreast of conditions, though deep down we thought this would be like other times. We had retreated to the basement to just return upstairs and go on with our normal routines.

As we are listening to the radio (tornado two miles south of Greensburg), I notice water dripping from the sewer line; that's weird I thought. As I went over to examine the area dripping, I checked out other pipes and they were totally dry. Is this imagination or is that drip getting bigger and dripping faster? Strange!!! We had a candle lit in case the electricity should go out. We wanted to save batteries in the flashlight for when absolutely needed. Just moments later, the electricity went off and I thought this is not a good sign. Using the flashlight, I turned off the water and gas valves. We had one hard wired phone in the house that was in the kitchen. We could hear it ringing for what seemed like a long time. We were praying it wasn't my mom calling to ask if it was all clear to come out now; since the siren had stopped when electricity went out. The phone Marquita brought to the basement was useless with no power and we had no signal on the cell phone. We smelled a strong smell of natural gas (strange since I'd turned the valve off) and I move quickly to blow the candle out and we huddled in a small area between the furnace and an old freezer.

We heard what sounded like huge hail hitting the house, then the windows popped, then the sound of a jet engine winding up for take off — right over our heads. Don't know if we'll ever get over the sound of the wind, objects hitting against the house, and the sound of glass breaking. Pressure in ears and my body became almost painful. I told my wife, "I love you, I love you, I love you". (At that moment that was all I could say so just kept repeating it). The whole time she is just whispering, "O Lord, O Lord, O Lord".

Then there was dust, plaster, and an insulation cloud engulfing the basement. The water was gushing in--no longer a little drip. Now there was an eerie quiet, just plain silence. We thanked God for our lives and then began to investigate. The trap door to the basement was blocked and there was no way I could lift it, even with Marquita's help. No way to get out, water was getting deeper and attempts to keep an area dry was impossible. We acknowledged the possibility of spending the night in our basement was now a reality.

Then yells of, "Ed, Ed, are you in there?" over and over came to our ears. Responding with screams of delight (hoping they could hear us), we yelled, "yes, we are in here — do you hear us?" Once established that we were heard, I gave directions on how to locate trap door so we could get out. Thank God for neighbors, they removed some debris and pushed the dryer back enough to prop open the door enough for us to crawl out.

We were not prepared for the horror awaiting us. We were overwhelmed as we surveyed (what we could see) the laundry area and our back porch area. It was so dark; the small amount of light from flashlights was not much to see by. When the lightning flashed, we were horrified by what little we could see of what was our home.

Shoes became the number one priority. There were glass, nails, and rubble everywhere. We got around to the front door of the house and were able to open it. Climbed over items we once used and appreciated which now looked like land-fill garbage. Marquita found her shoes right where they were left, though finding socks in the dark was a challenge. My shoes were on the floor behind my dresser, which was face-down on the floor. After retrieving shoes, we went outside to put them on. I was not too comfortable staying in the house as it did not look safe. We attempted to put shoes on but couldn't as they were full of glass and debris. We cleaned them out as best I could and finally got them on my feet; not an easy task when socks are wet.

First thoughts were, how are the kids (Mike, Jessica, and Aryca), and how's my mom? We have to go find them and see if they are ok. At first, we joked that we may need to spend the night at their house. With each step, our sense of reality was totally shattered. We were climbing over downed trees and power-lines, trying to get around cars, roofs, and who knew what all else. The farther we went things did not improve, unreal--unreal--unreal! Sense of urgency to find our daughter, granddaughter, son-in-law, and mom was overwhelming. Destruction around us was too massive to comprehend. We felt like we were moving in slow motion; we would see others in the same state. We/they were all asking, "have you seen...?" We were feeling so helpless, no answers of comfort for others or for ourselves. People were crawling out of total destruction. Scenes only familiar because of films and movies and television shows--THIS IS NOT SUPPOSE TO BE REALITY!!!

Our daughter and son-in-law's house was built of brick and mortar, I believed it could withstand anything---NOT! The north wall was partially gone--O my God, where are they? After climbing over much debris and through a broken window, we made it to their basement. The door was ajar, hollered for them and there was no answer--not even the dogs. I was not comfortable but went ahead and went down into the basement; was wet but intact. I found a cot with some bedding, looked like they had been there but were now gone. Maybe, they are looking for Mike's family or us, it appears they are ok.

We wandered around and then went up to Hwy. 54 and could see people moving to the east. We went to see what plans were or if there were any. We were told to go to Davis Park on the east side of town; that is where they wanted everyone to go. We, and many others, are headed east. Then we see others coming from east moving west--they were told to go to the

Dillon's lot — so we headed back. Sure enough, congregating had begun; it was so good to see familiar faces. We were continually asking if anyone had heard anything about Komotara, as that is where my mom lived; no one had heard anything. People everywhere, walking, some holding hands, some carrying bags or other items, yet we were all the same--confused, dazed, aimless, glazed eyes--no one seemed exempt.

By this time, rescue workers are arriving on the scene. Big lights are set up so we can see, yet it still seems like pandemonium; people still searching for family and friends, no one really knows what to do — lost, we are all lost.

Finally I tell Marquita to stay at Dillon's. I have to go find out about my mom. She says, "No way, I'm going with you. I'm not staying here without you, let's go." Off we went, trying to find the easiest way up to the apartments; there was no easy way. Rescue vehicles, people, debris, semi-trucks overturned blocking roads, cars, furniture, etc. etc. Horror upon horror with each block, can I wake up from this nightmare yet? We stumble our way south on Bay St.

We run into some people and ask about Komotara. They say they think it is ok. We breathe a sigh of relief and start walking a little slower. The wind had come up again and we are wet and cold. The cold wind in our faces is getting stronger; thought of another tornado strikes us with fear. There's no place to take cover; keep going it will be ok. It's dark up this way and our little flashlight isn't real bright, but we are thankful to have it with us.

Komotara looked fair from the top of the little rise. The walls, up on the NE corner and unit, looked intact. The next unit to the south was the one we were interested in. When we saw it, all we could do was gasp. It looked like a steam shovel had reached out into each apartment and ripped all the contents out into the front yard and street. Roofs were collapsed and walls separating units bent and twisted. Filled with dread, I shine my little flashlight into the interior of my mom's apartment and am hollering for her, I really can't see anything, can she have survived this? The area where the bathroom had been was totally collapsed. I'm trying to find a way to climb over and into the interior. Can't see well enough; just can't do it. Frantically trying to move debris, I hear a female voice behind me calling, "Are you Ed? Are you Ed?"

Having worked with people, with various mental illnesses who also resided at Komotara, I thought, please Lord. I can't handle this right now. I turned and answered, "Yes, it's Ed." They said, "Good, cause your mom is over here in the shelter. We helped her get out of the wind and the rain, we found her lying in the front yard amongst the tree limbs and debris, but she is ok."

Joy Unspeakable!!! Rescuers are going up and down streets--in some ways they seem as confused as we are--but we were able to get some help for the three ladies to be transported to Dillon's. I told the lady, "Please tell mom we will meet up with her at Dillon's."

On our way back to Dillon's, we stopped at our house. We wanted to try to get a jacket for each of us; maybe some dry socks. We knew that there was damage when we got shoes but really didn't know how bad it really was. As we are approaching the house, we are stopped by rescue workers and they ask who we are and we tell them, "This is our house, we want to get some jackets." They say, "No way, it isn't safe, we cannot allow you to go in there." They had big flashlights, jackets on, heavy boots, and hard hats and told us they could try to get jackets for us, just tell them where to look. Well, there was nothing there — so much for warmth. As he shined light into the kitchen it struck the refrigerator. I asked if he could get cigarettes for us from the freezer. So we walked away with those, but no dry socks and no jackets.

We then began our trek across town, needed a restroom and wanted to find Mike, Jessica, and Aryca. We went back to Mike and Jess's house. They still weren't there, but the restroom was useable — sorta. We wandered around some more and finally wound up at Dillon's again. We needed a restroom again. Thanks to Ray, Dillon's store manager, for allowing us to use the facility. Finally, we touched base with the kids at the parking lot--lots and lots of hugs, but where was mom. Mike, Jessica, and Aryca were not able to ride one of the buses leaving for shelters as they had three dogs with them, so they made other arrangements. Someone came and told me my mom was on the bus and I needed to get on it as it would be leaving shortly. So Marquita and I got on the bus and were taken to Haviland. Stories were shared by those on the bus and we were able to find out about other individuals that were ok; this was comforting to us.

Haviland was another place of confusion. People were everywhere, cots being set up, paperwork to fill out, and phone calls to make. Everyone was trying to make some arrangements and not really knowing what to do, medication lists being put together, etc.

Marquita and I were each allowed one phone call each. I called my brother in Pratt and she called her parents in Colorado. We were concerned that they would have seen news and be frantic. My brother was very concerned as they had been watching the storm and coverage on TV. Before we called him, they already knew we were ok as a good friend of ours was transported to Pratt and they were now at my brother's house. Marquita's folks were woke up by her call but were happy to hear from us nonetheless. Jessica had called them not too long after the storm (her cell phone was still working then). They had not seen anything on the news yet-- that only came later Saturday on national newscasts. Now the only thought is, what do we do now, what's the next step?

During this time, we are trying to rest, which isn't easy! Along came an angel to see us, she had red hair, a friendly voice of concern, and a plastic bag full of soft, dry, warm socks. The comfort of those socks on my feet will never be forgotten--Thank You. We tried to wrap a blanket around us to warm up and sleep, but sleep was not coming. Couldn't get my mom to lay down on a cot; she refused and said she was fine. I knew that she was very wet and cold and the hard bleachers had to be hard on her. I finally called my brother around 8a.m. and asked if he could come and get us. He sent his son to pick us up and take us to their home. We needed clean dry clothes so Marquita asked if someone could take her to the store; she's never looked so disheveled in public, but she was determined and on a mission.

Like so many of our neighbors from Greensburg we slept very little the days following the tornado, too many storms in the area with warnings, plus minds just didn't want to shut off. What do we do now? Where do we go from here? Same questions came over and over. Didn't help that we really had no comprehension of just how bad things in Greensburg were since we were not allowed back into town for three days. (Only saw media reports)

Once we were able to return to Greensburg, we saw just what the situation was concerning our home and the homes around us. We are thankful that our cat, Ryker, survived. He's been a part of our family for 14 years. After so many days, around 11 we think, The All Critters Rescue came and got our fish. We were astonished they were still alive. The tank was a total mess (I'd tried to scoop some of the debris out and added some food, but with no circulation it was not a pretty sight).

The story is told from Ed's perspective. Marquita concurs with most of the story. We only have differences in remembering sequence of events as they unfolded. This is no big deal; think most people have dealt with some of the same problems remembering time and sequence from that night, and the few days following that fateful night. All we know for sure is we, like so many others, traversed back and forth over parts of the town many times over that night with a total sense of unreality. Eyes seeing but the mind not fully able to comprehend all that we were looking at.

Many things have happened since the tornado. Attempting to put life back together, everyone does this in their own way. I want to share some thoughts. Disaster brought me to the realization that material things come and go. This was something I knew but hadn't experienced to this extent. Family and friends can be taken away just as quickly. The rut we live in becomes routine and comfortable. Routine and comfort are not bad things, but sharing our lives and showing the love and appreciation we have one for another is of absolute importance. We'll try not to let opportunities pass by will be my goal. As we have learned, we never know what event may come along and change everything.

Are tornados, included in all things? I believe so.

It has now been almost 15 months since that fateful day last May.

We have seen how quickly we can replace material things--houses, furnishings, clothes, cars, etc. We've also seen how relationships and friendships are not as easily replaced, family and friends are basic necessities in life. We cannot go back to the way things once were and yet a part of us longs to do just that, all the while knowing it simply is not possible.

There are many who chose not to rebuild but relocated to other areas, does this mean they cared any less about Greensburg than those who have rebuilt or will be rebuilding? NO. Most people had to make tough decisions and try to make the best decisions, at the time, for themselves and their families. We wish the best to each and every former resident of Greensburg, and best wishes to those already located in Greensburg and those with plans to return.

'And we know that in all things God works for the good of those who love him, who have been called according to his purpose.' (Romans 8:28 NIV)

submitted by: CHRIS UNRUH
OLD ADDRESS: 817 S. BAY • GREENSBURG, KS 67054
NEW ADDRESS: 314 W. 1ST, APT. #1 • PRATT, KS 67124

Looked Like a Bomb Had Dropped

On May 4, 2007, I went to work from 12 p.m. to 9 p.m. at Dillon's. It was a warm, muggy day and I thought to myself that it was going to rain. That isn't unusual for May.

I went to lunch from 4-5 p.m. and went home and watched the weather forecast. The weatherman was talking severe t-storms for all of the state of Kansas with the highest risk of severe weather in Greensburg. Knowing it was going to be bad, I went back to work from lunch and clocked in and started doing sanitation work at the store. I wanted to get caught up so I didn't have so much work to do later on after the store closed. That's when it really started looking stormy. As I carried my bags of trash outside the back door, it started thundering, lightning, and sprinkling. I went back into the store and took my floor machine out onto the sales floor and cleaned the whole floor. Just as I was pushing my machine back to the grocery backroom to be drained, the sirens went off. I told the Customer Service lady that we needed to go to the storm shelter which was the meat cooler. She followed me to the meat cooler. Just as we got to the cooler, that's when the tornado hit and the power went out. We held onto the door as the wind tried to blow it open. We heard loud thumps from things hitting the room. We waited quite a while before venturing out. When we walked out of the meat cooler, all of the store shelves were tipped over and half of the store was gone. We walked out the back door and it looked like a bomb had been dropped on the town. I couldn't believe my town was gone. There were people yelling for loved ones and we yelled back and said we were okay. Then we started gathering with the whole town in the parking lot. I walked over and started talking to people I knew and asked them if they were okay. I waited until the Red Cross came to pick up people to take them to a shelter that was set up at the Haviland gym. I helped injured people in ambulances that were there. The customer service lady and myself, along with a bunch of other people, walked down to the bar where some nurses and doctors were waiting to check on people who had scrapes and bruises. Then we walked back down to the Dillon's parking lot. Thats when the customer service lady's family picked up both of us and took us to her home in Haviland where I spent the night. I called my parents after we got to her house about 2:40 am Saturday morning and told them that I was okay. The next morning my parents drove all the way from Independence, Kansas. They stopped at Wal-Mart in Wichita to get some clothes for me because the clothes I had on was all that I had. On the Monday after the tornado, we had to wait awhile to get into town because of an anhydrous ammonia leak. When they let us in town on Monday, you had to go to the address that was on the windshield. The first place we went to was my apartment. I was able to salvage a lot of things from my apartment as my roof was still intact but I could see wood beams. After I got done with my apartment, I went to my folks house to help them. The roof of the house was gone with two walls blown out with only one wall hanging on by rebar and the ceiling in the hallway was beginning to separate. Dad put a two by four in place to keep it from separating even more. That was a long night I will never forget.

At the time this story was written, I am working at the Dillon's store in Pratt as the Assistant Grocery Manager.

Lighthouse Worship Center

Photo by Bruce Foster

United Methodist Church

Photo by Bruce Foster

submitted by: SUSAN WEST
216 W. GRANT • GREENSBURG, KS 67054

Everything is Gone

May 4, 2007 was like any other day until about 9:45 p.m. I was not in Greensburg the night of the tornado. I left town about 8:00 p.m. and headed for my mother's, Alice Boor, in Larned. My sister, Kim, was on her way from Sapulpa, OK to stay the weekend at my mother's. I originally had planned to just drop the kids off earlier in the day but decided I would stay Friday and go home in the morning. I would then get ready for my friend, Jaime's, wedding reception in Hays. I am so thankful Brett, 2 ½ months at the time, and I decided to stay in Larned. I can't imagine what it would have been like to have gone through the tornado with a baby; although, we were scared to death at my mother's.

We arrived at my mom and step-dad's (Tony) house about 9 p.m. Jason and I talked a few times on my drive to Larned. The kids were pretty upset because of all the lightning. Jason said there were tornadoes down by Protection. After getting the kids inside and settled down, we dished up ice cream and were getting ready to sit and watch TV when Jason called again. Jason asked me if I knew where mile marker 61 was. I didn't know. He said they were saying a tornado was on the ground and it was at mile marker 61 moving toward Greensburg. We did not have local channels at my mom's. So, we put on the weather channel. I will never forget Jason calling and telling me, "IT'S GONE! EVERYTHING IS GONE!" The reception was bad and I was trying to ask questions but I lost him. I remember I was telling my mom and sister that he better not be joking; simply because that would be mean. Then across the TV, they said, "Greensburg, KS has taken a direct hit"! I just fell to the floor and started to cry. I knew my family was ok but I just couldn't believe we lost our home; we had just purchased it two years prior. I started to think about my babies pictures. Everything else could be replaced. Of course, I was concerned for the lives of people in the path of the tornado.

Jason and I talked off and on; reception was so poor. Eventually, we had to go to my mother's utility room because there was a tornado coming our way. Kim and I had to run out in the rain and shut off the propane. I remember how scared we were. My kids were terrified. Tierra was worried about going to school and her friends. They had a million questions and I couldn't answer them. Tierra was very nauseated and at one time she was on the verge of vomiting. I was so scared that we would be hit and no one would know because we were so far in the country. The power kept going off and on. When it was on, we'd get on the computer and go to the news; hearing of all the devastation.

After the storms had past our area, we now had to worry about my brother, Billy, sister, Barbie, and my nieces and nephew who lived in Great Bend, KS. A tornado hit just east of where they lived. When they were out of danger, they came to mom's house. Billy and Barbie were going to watch the kids so we could go to Greensburg. However, Jason called and told me that this time I had to listen to him—I was not to come to Greensburg. He must not think I listen to him. I just had this urge to go and help. I knew there were people hurt and I had skills as a registered nurse to help. But, I listened to my husband and stayed put. I think we all laid down about 5:30 a.m. I was awake at 7:30 a.m. I talked to my dad again and let him know what was going on. I found it interesting that my dad usually watches the weather, but for some reason, he wasn't watching that night. I had called him several times throughout the night and informed him of what I knew. He called family and let them know we were alive but our home was destroyed.

Jason showed up with Buddy about 9 a.m. It was nice to see him after the night of hell. I didn't like being separated but I am glad my children didn't experience the storm first hand.

The aftermath was enough. We thought we were going to get into town on Saturday but didn't. We went to the Haviland gym and registered and checked in with the insurance company. We were so happy to see people and find out how everyone was doing.

We stayed Saturday at my mom's and went through another adventure. Saturday night brought more storms. The rumble of the storms started and needless to say Jason was not staying in the country. So, he had all ten of us load in vehicles and head to the Larned Police Station where my step-dad was working. We took shelter there. After the storm passed, we could not get down the dirt road to my mom's. So, we stayed in a hotel. It was another very long night.

We finally got to see Jason's parents, Mary Jean and Ken, on Sunday. We were all so glad to see each other. We stayed with Jason's aunt and uncle, Gary and Linda Brehm, in Pratt. We were there nearly two weeks until we moved to Priscilla Brack's rental house. We were thankful to have a place to go. Priscilla has taken us in and treated us like family. We appreciate all she has done.

So many people helped us after the disaster; from Jason's company, family, friends and complete strangers. Our neighboring towns were so helpful. Thank you all!

We now are getting our lives back to "normal"; if there is such a thing. Our new home is being built by Charles Wadel and his sons and should be finished by the first of the year (2009). I am grateful that we had a home to live in and did not have to live in a FEMA trailer but I will not miss the drive.

Greensburg is home to us and that is why we chose to stay. I think we have a good school system and I love working at the Kiowa County Memorial Hospital. No, Greensburg is not the same but it's the people that make Greensburg home; not the buildings.

submitted by: CHRISTINA THORNOCK
OLD ADDRESS: 219 N. WALNUT • GREENSBURG, KS 67054
NEW ADDRESS: 410 N. IUKA • PRATT, KS 67124

It Will Be Home Forever

On Friday, May 4th, I got off work around 4:30 that afternoon. All I could think about was I knew this weekend had to be better than the last weekend I had off. I went and picked up my daughter from daycare and went home. We lived with my parents at the time at 219 N. Walnut due to other circumstances in my life. Dad and mom were coming home that evening. They had been gone all week somewhere for mom's job with Duckwall's. I know that it was hot that day. When my parents got home, it seemed strange outside. We ate dinner and just settled in for the night. Dad went to bed. Mom, Isabel and I were just hanging out watching the weather. I forget what time it was when my brother called and told us we needed to get to the basement. We told him we were going as we stood at the front door and watched the rain and hail. Then all of a sudden, it got really calm and it clicked with mom and I. The signs were there that you had always heard of. I don't know who said it first or if it was said at all but we headed to the basement. I got Isabel some shoes to put on, but I never thought to get other clothes for her. She was playing dress up earlier and had on my slip and shirt. Mom woke up dad and we told him to get to the basement now. I told mom I was going to get my purse and cell phone and a box that had Isabel's birth certificate and other important papers. As I grabbed everything, I remembered her shot record was in another place. Just as I reached down for it, the lights went off. Mom told me to hurry as she lit the way with a flashlight. Isabel was hesitant to go down the stairs and I understood as I hated basements. I always have. Even though I went first, I knew we had to drag her down them. Mom came down and dad last. Dad did not shut the door or it didn't stay shut; (I am not sure which) but he no more got down there and it started. The three of us made a circle around Isabel. She was scared and crying. We prayed for God's protection and started singing "Old McDonald" to keep her calm. I don't remember my ears popping. I just was focused on Isabel. I don't know how she breathed as the three of us was around her so tight. I was scared to death and I just knew that the house was going to fall in on us. It was loud but the funny thing is that it just didn't sound like the whole house would be destroyed.

After what seemed like forever, we went upstairs. The bathroom at the top of stairs was a mess but all the walls were there. We looked in the kitchen and we could tell we could not get out the front or back of the house. It was blocked by all of our belongings. We thought we could jump out of the kitchen window that was now gone but we worried that there would be glass on the ground and it was a big drop. We realized when we returned that the walls on the north side of the house were gone and all we had to do was walk over the bed and make our way through the debris to the street. Isabel cried and was scared but once we got to the street she was fine. She was a trooper for the rest of the night.

We wondered what had happened to Roscoe, my dog, that I'd had for eleven years. As we walked down the street, we called to neighbors to see if everyone was ok. Isabel yelled to Miss Missy, one of the teachers at preschool, to make sure she was ok. She lived two houses down from us. She yelled to Isabel that she was fine. Isabel made the comment that there were no more houses to have sleepovers at (out of the mouths of babes). We walked to the highway not even sure where it was. There was unbelievable destruction of the whole town; my home, the place where I grew up. What was going to happen now? We looked like zombies. Once at the highway, we started heading west. Someone said there was another tornado coming. We panicked. A man came by and said there was no tornado. He said to go to the highway department and wait. That is just what we did. On the way, we walked by Dillon's in the dark. It didn't look so bad. Until later, I saw just how bad it was. I had worked there fourteen years and I thought I would be there fourteen more (little did I know). We saw friends and co-workers but today I can't tell you who they were. When we reached our destination, we were some of the first ones there. We just stood for awhile still trying to use our cell phones to let my brother and sister in Pratt know where we were. My cousin, Brian, got through on my phone and asked me if I'd seen his parents, Verita and Ron Larrick. It was then that all the names of people came rushing to me. Were they ok? Were they alive? People slowly started to trickle in. Then they setup a triage unit. I finally saw my aunt and uncle and they told us my brother and sister was looking for us. Someone else told my mom that my sister had found my dog. We waited and waited. Finally, I told my parents that I was going to look for them. As I started to walk to the highway, someone caught my eye. It was my brother, Jason. With the look of worry and relief, I hugged him hard. I was so glad to see him. Angela, my sister, was nearby. Again, I never wanted to let her go. What a bonus; she had my dog! We wanted to go to Pratt and stay with Jason but how do we get there? About that time, my cousin walked up and had a vehicle to transport us.

On the way, all the vehicles coming into Greensburg was an awesome sight. All the people who came that night were unbelievable. Whenever I hear people say that people don't help one another, I always say, "You weren't in Greensburg, KS on May 4, 2007."

It has been a year and a half since that horrific night. Isabel and I are living in Pratt, about three blocks away from my brother and his family. Mom and Dad are here too. They live about four blocks from my sister and her family, on the other side of Main Street from my house. Our life is different. I lived in Greensburg most of my life; that is all I've known. So, the adjustments have not always been easy. Thanks to the people I work with and the people of Pratt, it feels a little bit like home. I get asked two to three times a week if I'm going back to Greensburg. With a sad heart, I say no. The job I once had is no longer there. Most of my friends and co-workers are also gone. I do see some of the customers still in Pratt at Dillon's. It makes me happy because I think I miss them the most.

My beloved Greensburg is gone; never to be the same again. Our little sleepy town is gone. What is coming I'm sure will be great but sadly it will be different. For all the people who think I abandoned Greensburg or think of me as a traitor (I have been called that), they should know that a piece of me will always be there; it will be home forever. So, don't forget about us who did not return. It was a hard decision to make. Maybe one day I won't cry when I go back thinking of all that we have lost.

submitted by: **BRANDON AND ALYSSA BROWN**
OLD ADDRESS: 117 W. COLFAX • GREENSBURG, KS 67054
NEW ADDRESS: 522 N. JACKSON • PRATT, KS 67124

Don't Take Any Day For Granted

I am Alyssa Brown. My mom and dad are Sandy and Brian Foster. My sister is Erica Foster and my niece is Kaylee Pitts. My husband is Brandon Brown and our son is Jason Brown. We also have a daughter named Christina, who wasn't with us at the time of the tornado.

A tornado 1.7 miles wide hit our 1.7 mile wide town of Greensburg, where I had lived for almost 21 years of my 22 year life. It hit on the eve of May 4th, 2007.

Dad's birthday was May 3rd and we had thrown a birthday party for him at our house on 117 West Colfax Avenue the weekend previous to May 3rd. Little did we know, that it would be the last time our whole family would be together in our little cottage style home. We had a very special time, and I will always look back on

that party with a smile...a sad smile. It is hard for me to write this all down.

The devastation and trauma will always be with us. The sadness will never leave. This was the biggest tornado reported in eight years. It may have been the biggest tornado in world history.

We had planned on surprising dad with a weekend get-away to Wichita to see Spiderman III at the Warren Theater. We were going to spend the night at the Hilton Garden Hotel that had just opened...on the infamous weekend of May 5th and 6th.

Brandon and I were packing for the trip Friday evening, May 4th. I was hurriedly doing laundry laying it out on our new sectional as I always did so it wouldn't wrinkle. Brandon had been watching the

Brandon and Alyssa Brown House Before

Photo by Erica Foster

weather conditions on the television. Brandon said that we had to get over to Mom and Dad's house because the whistle was going to blow for a tornado warning. Brandon knew I was too freaked out to get into our small cellar and would be more likely to go to Mom and Dad's basement. I was so annoyed. Tornado sirens never meant anything in Greensburg Kansas. I had gone to the basement many times in my lifetime and nothing ever happened. I had a lot to do to get ready to go on our trip, but, better safe than sorry.

Brandon and I loaded Jason up and dashed to Mom and Dad's two story Victorian style home on 122 West Grant Avenue. Brandon said the tornado siren was going to go off; just at that moment it started going off on cue. All of us headed to the basement. My sister Erica and her daughter Kaylee were living with Mom and Dad so they were with us also.

Dad located a spot in a separate room where he thought his family would be the safest while I argued with Brandon not to go upstairs to look for a flash light. We all sat down on the floor amidst Christmas decorations and boxes of things in storage. Erica had a file cabinet next to her on the right. I remember commenting that mom's wedding dress was behind me and stopping to stroke it. Erica had Kaylee on her lap and I was trying to corral the three dogs and keep them near me. Brandon had a hold on Jason and was making me increasingly anxious the way he was pacing instead of sitting. I had to beg Brandon and Dad both to sit down. Brandon crouched on the floor next to me with Jason sheltered in his arms.

Dad refused to go into the room with us and stayed in a separate room. He had assessed the situation and decided that if we were trapped in that room, someone would need to be on the outside of it to dig us out. I desperately begged him to join us but he stubbornly stood his ground.

Brandon brought our digital camera to take pictures of the funnel clouds so we used it to amuse ourselves and took pictures of each other to keep calm. Brandon also had our cell phone in the pocket of his wind pants. We were singing the Happy Birthday Song to Grandpa to keep Kaylee calm and found candles from Erica's wedding and a lighter, so we lit them and let Kaylee blow them out at the end of each song.

The siren had been blowing for at least twenty minutes, when suddenly it died. We knew it wasn't because the threat was over. The lights flickered and went out. We had lit two candles, but decided to blow them out in case something were to happen (we didn't want to be on fire on top of everything else).

We sat in darkness, paralyzed with fear. "Daddy, get in here NOW!" I yelled over and over, but he stayed put.

Dad knew the basement wasn't going to hold. He had been thinking for months of putting in a storm shelter. He even had a tree removed in the back yard, fearing that it would fly into the basement and crush us if we were in a tornado. Mom was too claustrophobic to get into a storm shelter or cellar, so Dad had dropped the idea. The basement was made of nothing more than mere plaster; built as an afterthought after the house had already been erected. The project was done over 100 plus years ago. Dad knew it wasn't fit for what was coming.

We started hearing sounds of siding being ripped off of the house, and massive amounts of glass being shattered. "WHAT IS THAT SOUND?" Erica half whispered in a panic. Mom knew we were under the tornado, and she jumped to her feet and yelled "NO!!!" At that moment, the ceiling and walls caved in and knocked mom down to her knees.

The noises intensified. Then I felt a strong wind blowing back my hair as if it was trying to rip it from my scalp and a roar as if we were on a roller coaster. My ears began to pop over and over

and over again and it felt like my ear drums were exploding. It felt like a truckload of dirt was being dumped on us. It was in our eyes, mouths, and hair. I felt a metal bar rake down my back, scooting me forward. I began to frantically pray that we wouldn't be buried alive.

My thoughts were still on my father. I knew that if we were in the safest room in the basement and it was this bad, than how bad was it for Dad? "DADDY! DADDY!" I screamed and screamed into the wind that immediately sucked my breath out and silenced my screams. Dad's dead, Dad's dead!!!! This was racing through my mind. Then I heard my sister next to me screaming "JESUS SAVE MY BABY!!!!" And that's when it became real for me. I began saying the Lord's prayer and also asking God to accept my family into his Kingdom. I didn't think there was any way we were going to survive, so I was praying we would all have quick deaths instead of being buried alive. Reality struck that Dad wasn't the only one in danger-we all were. "MOMMY!" I screamed. "I'm here" I heard her muffled reply. "BRIAN?" I heard her yell, but we couldn't hear him if he was yelling back.

"Is everyone ok?" Mom yelled once the wind stopped. "I've been hit on the head but I think I'm ok", yelled Brandon, who was next to me on my left. Jason was screaming his head off in his arms. "I've been hit in the back but I think I'm ok," I yelled. "Can you get out?" We were all pinned and Brandon was the first to try and break free so he could help tunnel the rest of us through. He pulled the cell phone from his pocket and used it for light. He saw nails protruding from the board that had struck him on the head, and it was still only about an inch from his face.

I shoved the three dogs through the narrow path I saw first. I attempted to crawl out with Kaylee, and had to wriggle out of my shoes to free myself and begin crawling on my belly through a small opening. Kaylee was paralyzed with fear and wouldn't move so we inched our way back and Brandon tried to go with Jason next.

I heard Daddy's voice!!! He was right, — we did need his help to get out, and he was clearing us a path. Brandon got himself and got the kids out and continued working on clearing a way out with Dad. Then I went through and Erica was last. I remember calling back to her to be careful; the hot water heater was on the ground and we had no choice but to slither over the top of it. It was still really hot and it burned us as we went over it. There were broken Christmas ornaments, glass and nails everywhere. All the pipes to the house were busted, plus it was raining violently, and our tunnel was filling with water and we knew we had to hurry.

Once we were out of that room and were able to stand, we still had to somehow make it out of the basement. We were all in shock and I stared at Dad as if he were a ghost who was going to disappear. I couldn't believe he had made it and was standing in front of me. (He later recapped to us that he too, had been knocked to the ground by the caving ceiling and walls and things flying around the room and had to fight his way out).

We briefly considered using our cell phone to call for help, but immediately realized that it was probably a disaster all over town, with many people needing help. The house had been picked up and thrown at least eight feet from its foundation. The opening that used to be the top of the basement stairs was now a tight, steep crawlspace that we would have to crawl through to get to safety. The basement stairs were covered in heavy debris and we had to get hand and footholds on whatever we could.

We thought about having the smallest adult go first and go for help if the others couldn't get out, but the house was continuing to cave all around us and it wasn't safe for anyone to stay there for long.

I started the climb first, and I was not brave. I was shaking from complete horror from what we'd been through and knowing that it wasn't over and we could still be killed. "Daddy!" I cried in my misery. "I'm here, baby girl."

I finally made it up and out and they handed Jason up to me. He was about 10 months old and weighed about twenty five pounds. Erica and Kaylee came up next. We couldn't see except for when lightning struck. The smell of wet wood was over-powering. We could see the total devastation through the lightning, and that there was nothing left of the precious home we grew up in. Our legs were wobbling and we were both shaking from adrenaline. The wind was blowing around 200 miles per hour and the storm was not over. It was hailing big chunks of ice that felt like glass when it hit our skin with the force of the wind. We yelled to each other to take refuge in the garage, but there was no garage. Then Erica yelled to get into her car, which had all the windows busted out. We got in and huddled over our babies but it wasn't much shelter, and we were sitting on broken glass. We were both barefoot, and we couldn't see where we were stepping; both children were screaming and screaming.

When we saw Brandon, we got out of the car and tried to figure out where to go. We were standing in what used to be Mom and Dad's driveway. We saw Dad's van turned over on it's side all smashed with the light on inside of it. It was pitch dark--no street lights. Brandon yelled we should go to the hospital, which was two blocks away. So we trudged onward. I kept looking back to see if Mom and Dad were behind us. I finally saw them coming. The wind blew so hard we struggled to keep both feet on the ground. Our babies were being sucked out of our arms, and I had to give Jason to Brandon. (I am in awe of my sister, who literally saved her daughter's life that night by her determination and physical strength).

What we saw in the lightning on our way to the hospital was like a scene from a movie or an XBOX game. We saw smashed, overturned vehicles, arcing power lines and busted up trees. It was so surreal. Brandon kept telling me not to look around. I tried to look away, but I couldn't. I was totally awestruck. I watched as a car door got ripped off by the wind and sucked up into the air, twirling as it went so high I couldn't see it anymore. I was afraid it would come back down and kill us, but I never saw it again.

We finally reached the hospital and by that time there were other townspeople around us with their dogs and flash lights. Mom had grabbed Bobby, her black teacup poodle on the way out of the basement, but the other two dogs were still trapped in the collapsing basement.

The hospital smelled like gasoline and was half gone. The townspeople were demanding that we all go to its basement, and our whole family hesitated. (We didn't want to go through that again!) We finally went, but mom and dad were very hesitant. "Just get down there, girls," dad said. The ceilings were caved in and there were tiles dangling off in many places and shattered glass all over the stairs. The basement was like a nightmare.

Our bloody feet coated the floors along with many other people's blood and there was urine and dog feces all over the floor.

The nurses were incredible. They stayed on duty and treated people with great concern and thoughtfulness. They brought us diapers, drinking water and dry hospital gowns to change into. One nurse even gave me a pair of shorts so that my backside wouldn't show. They walked around treating wounds, not knowing if their own families were safe. They had ambulances and a school bus coming to take victims to the Dillon's parking lot where there was a triage. They also had a pick up truck, which is what our family eventually rode away in after two and a half hours of waiting. Daddy was so sweet about his worries about our bare feet. We had sat so long watching people being wheeled in and out on stretchers, groaning in pain and bleeding. Even though the power was out,

there was an annoying buzzer that was ear-splittingly loud going off and red lights were flashing...sending our nerves through the roof. We tried to stay calm as we thought about all the people we knew in Greensburg and wondered if they were still alive.

We were relieved to see Holly, our hairdresser, who was ok and we hugged her tight. Rocky Prebble was the first person I saw when I first got down the stairs and he was so nice and caring. He asked if we were all ok and if our animals were ok. I couldn't honestly answer the animal question. I cried and cried thinking about Ringo, my teacup Chihuahua, who was still trapped under the house without food or water. Also, trapped was Prissy, my sister's 14 year old terrier, who was blind and going deaf with arthritis.

When they finally called our names, we drove off in the back of the pick up. We tried to look around at the town on our way to Dillon's. It was such an incredible mess that we couldn't identify many buildings.

Once at Dillon's, I remember the pastor, who married Brandon and I, Marvin George, helping me out of the back of the truck. I was so happy to see him, and told him I was worried about him and was so glad he was okay.

There was a standing section for those who were not harmed and a sit-down section for people who needed an ambulance for medical attention. We were headed to the stand-up section, but our former co-worker, Connie Dawson, came over and demanded we sit and got mom a wheelchair (and we're very grateful that she did!). As we sat waiting on the ambulance, we saw news cameras recording us and saw we were being photographed. The photo of us sitting there would later be plastered on the front page of many newspapers all over the U.S., and went on to win the Kansas Press Association photo of the year award for 2007.

Dad didn't think he was injured enough to ride in the ambulance and that it was more urgent for someone else to go. We all begged Dad to come with us and pretty soon Connie came back over and got him talked into getting into the ambulance (our hero!)

Dad had to lie on a gurney in the middle of the ambulance with his legs strapped down when we began moving. He didn't enjoy that much. There were two male responders in the ambulance. One took our information and one treated our wounds with antiseptic and bandages. There was an elderly woman in the ambulance with us named, Opal, who couldn't remember much and had a head wound gushing blood down her face and cut up hands. She was clutching her purse, which was covered in blood. They wrapped her purse in a bio hazard bag.

One responder gave Jason and Kaylee teddy bears. They had to give me a barf bag, since I was very nauseated and I dry heaved all the way to the Pratt Hospital, 35 miles from Greensburg. When the ambulance doors opened, we stood up and came face to face with my handsome, smiling cousins, Terry and Jeremy, who live in Hutchinson! They had come looking for us and were on their way into the hospital when they saw the ambulance and waited to see if we were in it. Sure enough!

They were a sight for sore eyes. And then we saw Jeremy's beautiful wife, Haleola was there too. Many of our wonderful family members started coming out of the wood work to support us. Brandon's Dad, Ricky, and his wife, Diana, and her sister, Dottie, came, as well as Brandon's mother, Pamela, and her husband, Tim. They supported us financially and emotionally. My cousin Angela, her husband Steve, and their three beautiful children, Denton, Lacie and Alexis Branscom came to the hospital that night, as well as mom's sister Linda and her husband Mel Osner. (Linda, Mel and Terry were kind enough to dog-sit for mom and dad's poodle!).

Brandon's sisters, Erica Moody and Sarah Booth, came up to baby-sit Jason for us while we cleaned up our properties. All of our family members were so gracious and so appreciated. They bought us clothes and took care of all our needs until we were able to get to our banks. Haleola and Jeremy gave us tons of clothes. Pam and Tim, Ricky and Diana all let us borrow their vehicles. Steve and Angela even got us a moving truck when the time was right. Ricky, Mel and Linda, Terry and Jeremy, Haleola, Steve and Angela's family came to help us clean up our lots. Kaylee's father, Tim Pitts also came to help us and he bought us nice clothes for the kids. Brandon's cousin, Paula, sent us the sweetest letter. Brandon's Granny, Austinetta Brown, now deceased, called us daily and prayed her little heart out for us. The Church of Christ in Sylvia allowed us to stay in their church parsonage while we cleaned up our lots. We had many family members and friends, churches and businesses in Childress Texas raising money for us. There was a grocery bagger in Dillon's in Hutchinson named Danny Elam where my Aunt Linda shopped and when she told him about our family, he made calls and rounded up clothes for all of us, making sure they were the right sizes. We are still so touched and impressed with what Danny did for us. We are tremendously blessed to have such a great family.

Mom and I had x- rays, but were found to be just fine. Brandon and dad both refused to let anyone examine them. They were determined that someone worse off than them could have the doctor's attention.

None of us had lasting physical defects, but for awhile Mom and I both had scars in the shape of an upside-down triangle in the same spots on our left shoulders-the shape of a tornado!

It was an agonizing three days before they would let us back into the town of Greensburg to come after our animals and possessions. We saw ourselves on TV, sitting on the bench at the Dillon's triage waiting for the ambulance on the news, just before they panned over to a clip of the President of the United States, declaring Greensburg a disaster area. We stayed at the Value Inn Motel in Hutchison for over a week.

When we finally could get back into Greensburg, we called for our dogs. My tiny teacup Chihuahua popped his head up from under the house when he heard my voice. I had to coax him up over the top of many large piles of rubble to get him over to me. It was so wonderful to have him back! (My sister's dog, Prissy, was later found at the animal rescue shelter that had been set up in Greensburg). Both dogs had cuts, but were ok!

I'll never forget Dad picking his motorcycle up from the rubble of his home of thirty years. He lovingly brushed off the seat, and rode it around the block for the last time.

Two weeks from the tornado, we found a gorgeous home in Pratt that was big enough to meet all of our needs. Mom and Dad bought it and we moved into it together. Brandon and I later found our own dream home in Pratt and with both joy and sadness, moved out. We are trying to get back to being ourselves. Mom still needs to purchase a piano. This is the longest she hasn't played since she was seven years old.

Dad finally got his motorcycle back on November 1st, 2008. We feel like a member of the family has come home. Mom still has her tornado scars, just as we all do (except our scars are on the inside).

We are the closest family that you'll ever find. We don't take any day for granted, and we cherish each other. Our hearts are broken for the families in Greensburg that lost loved ones, some of which we had known personally.

We owe a large debt of gratitude to the many people who helped us, and to our Lord and Savior, Jesus Christ, who is and always will be an awesome God!!!

Kwik Shop   *Photo by Stacy Barnes*

submitted by: **RAY AND WILMA MCCHRISTIAN**
OLD ADDRESS: 606 S. SPRUCE • GREENSBURG, KS 67054
NEW ADDRESS: 215 E. 37TH AVE. • HUTCHINSON, KS 67502

How Blessed We Are

On May 4, 2007, Ray and I had just returned home from an overnight trip to Oklahoma. Ray was on the telephone to Calvin (our son) in Hutchinson about 9:00 p.m. when the tornado siren started to sound. I'm sure my first thought was, "Oh here we go again!" I had never gotten too excited about a torndo siren as our human mindset is that "it will never happen to me." But the siren kept going and going so Ray finally told Calvin he'd better get off the phone and we turned on the TV. This was the first realization to me that this could be serious. We were tuned to the channel with Merrill Teller, the meteorologist. He was displaying the radar screen with the tornado at the Kiowa-Comanche county line. The image was a very large purple blob and I realized it must be a huge storm. It was starting to hail some, so I got the keys to our old 1991 Lumina that was sitting out by the curb. We always kept the keys to that car in a dish on the kitchen counter. My plan was to move the car up in the yard under the big maple tree to protect it from the hail. But when I reached the garage door, the lightning was ferocious, flashing every few seconds. I thought, "this would be stupid to get struck by lightning over a sixteen year old car." So, I dropped the keys in my pocket and did not go outside. As it turned out later, it was a good thing I had those keys in my pocket.

Back in the house, I decided I'd better get some clothes to the basement so I went to the closet and grabbed an arm load. I also saw the suitcase from the Oklahoma trip and a shoe bag with my better shoes. So, we grabbed those and took them to the basement. Ray saw me getting some clothes, so he got an extra pair of jeans and couple of shirts. I thought of getting a few more things like the old kerosene lamp from our mantel over the fireplace but thought, "Oh the more things I drag to the basement, the more things I'll just have to take back upstairs and put away later." Meanwhile, Ray got flashlights from the two good vehicles "safe" in the garage. I'm so glad he did as I would have not thought of them as they are so essential. Periodically, we'd look at the TV in the basement and Merrill was urging everyone to seek underground cover. The last I remember hearing him, he was stating the tornado was six miles south of Greensburg and he said, "Its big, and its moving slow." An inner voice told me that this time we were going to get hit. In the basement, we got two large cushions off a sofa and Ray handed me his old hard hat from Panhandle Eastern. He also grabbed his old motor cycle helmet! They were both stored on a shelf nearby where we planned to stay during the storm. We put those on and laughed as we looked at each other. We got back in a narrow storage area and squatted down low with our helmets on and sofa cushions held over us and waited. Suddenly, the lights went off and sirens stopped blowing.

Soon pressure started building up in our ears like when you are driving up a mountain really fast. I remember thinking, "This is not good." The pressure kept increasing and worsening until I was fearful that my eardrums would explode. I said a little prayer to God and asked that I wouldn't be deaf permanently. Ray and I did not talk a lot but he did communicate that his ears were feeling the same way.

Finally, my ears popped open and I was so thankful to be rid of that horrible pressure and I was able to hear. Then I thought, "If I hear the sound of a train, we're really getting hit!" So I kept listening for that sound but never heard it. Next, we started hearing loud thuds on the floor above us. It sounded like there were several people with sledge hammers hitting the floor above us or boulders being dropped. At one point, I heard a clunk right above my head and rusty wet gravel sprayed on my neck. I knew we were sitting directly under a half-bathroom and I thought, "Oh, I don't want anything from those pipes on my neck!" So, I took a large plastic flower pot sitting next to me and put that over my head too. Later, we noticed a cast iron sewer pipe had broken near us. Helmets were a good idea after all!

Finally, all the noise stopped and we waited long enough that we were sure the storm was over. We got up and with flashlights walked around to the stairwell to go upstairs. That area was full of debris to the point that we couldn't get up the steps. So, we pulled some of the stuff on down into the basement and Ray got up far enough that he could pick some up and throw it out the top. It all consisted of sheet rock, small tree limbs, broken lumber with nails, electrical wiring, etc. I kept asking Ray if he could see the piano as he made his way farther up the stairs, as it sits in the living room near the stairwell. I had always been wary that in the event of a tornado that piano might fall through the floor. It was an old upright from the 1920's and weighed several hundred pounds. I was worried that it might be up there in an unstable situation and could still fall in on us.

Ray was finally able to get up the stairs far enough to shine his flashlight around. He said, "Wilma, our house is gone!" I thought, "Oh, he just can't see very well with a little flashlight." I really didn't believe him. But I came up right after him and sure enough, we were standing in open air with the sky above us and nothing around us. There was not one wall left, no furniture, no bathroom or kitchen fixtures, and as we discovered later, even the carpet was stripped from the floor. The piano was lying out in the back yard about thirty-five feet from where it once was. We were asked days later by an insurance claim agent how long it took us to come to grips with the fact that our house was gone. Both Ray and I said without hesitation, "within seconds." The same thing happened a few years earlier to another couple in rural Kiowa County from a tornado. Their house was literally swept away with nothing left. At that time, I looked at my house and tried to imagine it all being gone in a matter of minutes. So, my thought was, "This time it happened to us." My thoughts of regret were to lose the irreplaceable items like my dad's fiddle. He, my sister and I played music together many hours while I was growing up. Also, lost was a decorative table Ray's father had made. Calvin's beautiful coffee table that he made in high school shop class was destroyed. Many other things that were lost were handmade by other family members or dated back to our grandparent's time.

All that remained of Ray's workshop was the concrete slab and some more rubble.

Our next thoughts were of our neighbors. With thankful hearts, we started seeing many of them out in the street with their flashlights. Soon the immediate neighbors were accounted for and John Colclazier and Ray headed north to check on people on Spruce Street. John David Colclazier and I headed over to Carriage House and were thankful to hear that they were all ok. The rest of the night is a little blurred. I made it over to Alice Burch's and couldn't believe that her land line telephone was working. We used her phone to notify our relatives that we were alright. A few more people made a call on Alice's phone and then it went dead. Most cell phones were not working reliably. It was difficult to get through the streets as there were trees, power lines, broken poles and boards with nails blocking the way. We made our way through flooded streets and over fallen trees detouring up into people's yards, trying to find a less difficult path through the area. A neighbor, who was a nurse, and I made our way to the hospital and stayed awhile, but they seemed well organized and were already evacuating all the patients and clients. We then made our way to Dillon's parking lot. I do remember being indescribably thirsty. I have never been a water drinker and couldn't believe I was so thirsty. I was thirsty immediately after the tornado and it lasted until morning. There were cases of bottled water at the Dillon's parking lot and I was so thankful for a drink.

I had really thought we would just be there until morning before help came. I couldn't believe how soon men were there with bulldozers, big trucks, etc. clearing the streets for emergency vehicles.

After the streets were cleared enough that you could get through them, I remember dogs running as fast as they could as if they didn't know what they were doing. If you happened to be standing in their way, they just glanced off you and raced on down the street.

Around 3:00 a.m., Ray and I met up again back at our lot as we called it by then. We were tired and decided to rest on the sofas that we had in the basement. Rain was seeping through the flooring, and the basement was getting wet. We rested until around 6:00 a.m. and then came up out of the basement and were surprised to find a law enforcement officer on our lot. He seemed surprised to see us too. He told us that the town had been evacuated and that we would have to leave too. So, we got our overnight bag and a few belongings from the basement. The two good vehicles were still where the garage had been but were badly damaged. They were later totaled by the insurance company. Ray looked at the Lumina sitting at the curb and said he thought it would run if we could pull the tree branches away from it. My first thought was that we didn't have a key for it. But then I remembered the key in my pocket! All the windows on the driver's side were blown out and the windshield was badly cracked. The inside was matted with crumbled glass, twigs, insulation, splintered lumber and leaves. But, it started up and we were able to

drive it to Mullinville. When we got to the school gym, I couldn't believe there was food and coffee ready for us and Mullinville people were there registering us on a computer. That coffee smelled so good!! We spent Saturday night with our preacher and then moved to a friend's house south of Mullinville. We gratefully stayed there seven weeks and shared the house most of that time with Jim and Karen Smith. One night about ten days after the Greensburg's tornado, all of us were awakened by a NOAA radio broadcast. That alert stated there was another tornado in our area. We all spent about an hour under the pool table in the basement. Luckily, it passed us.

Monday morning, we were able to drive back into town; through the check point and back to our lot. During the next couple of weeks, we had countless people spending countless hours helping us clean up our area, salvaging items from the yard and hauling it to various places of storage. I hesitate to mention names because I'll never get them all listed or remember them all. Our church family at the Church of Christ at Mullinville did so much for so many families. Thanks for all the hours you spent serving meals and operating the distribution center. I extend a big thank you to those who brought their strong backs and their pickups. One friend used his bobcat to shove most of our debris out to the curb.

I would also like to recognize the emergency crews from the surrounding towns who were there so promptly. Our gratitude is to all the churches who had kitchens in Greensburg and fed thousands. We were impressed with the aid provided by the Salvation Army and American Red Cross. Both organizations were there with water, food, gas money, and other supplies. A thank you also is granted to the Kansas National Guard and all the DOT personnel who spent weeks clearing the debris and hauling it away. The life of every person in Kiowa County was affected.

With stunned minds, we began trying to decide what to do next. Ray did not have the mental and emotional energy to rebuild. I clung to the thought of rebuilding for awhile, but to be honest, the last thing I'd ever wanted to do was build a house. The countless decisions that have to be made with building under normal circumstances is daunting to me, and I have no designing or decorating skills. So with heavy hearts, we looked at Pratt and Hutchinson for a house. We found a home and shop area that fit our needs in Hutchinson and we could be near our son, daughter-in-law and two grandchildren. So after forty years in Greensburg for Ray and thirty-five years for me, we made a move we never thought we'd ever make. We have found Hutchinson people to be very friendly and are getting busier with local activities here. We will probably always have an empty spot in our hearts for the people of Kiowa County. We remind each other still how blessed we are that neither of us was hurt and that we had each other to go through this transition together.

submitted by: JASON WEST

216 W. GRANT • GREENSBURG, KS 67054

We Will All Remember

It was around 8:00 p.m. when I got home that night. I had been listening to the weather band in my truck all afternoon about the severe thunderstorms building up in Oklahoma and moving to the north. I was determined to get my Dodge Mega-cab into the shed before the large hail and possible tornadoes arrived.

After putting my pickup under the protection of the shed, I walked over to the van where my wife, Susan, my daughter, Tierra, and my sons, Bo and Brett were waiting. They were going to Susan's mom's house in Larned, to stay the night, and to see Susans' sister, Kimmie. As I kissed them all goodbye, the eerie black storm clouds were fast approaching. We could hear this continuous, deep, rumbling roar of thunder off in the distance. I told Susan that something was going to happen and if the storms were bad up there to just stay in her mom's utility room downstairs.

OKAY! The pickup is in the shed, the dogs are fed and the family is on the road. PEACE AND QUIET! But not for long! The TV said that there was a tornado at the Comanche/Kiowa county line moving to the northeast. My mom called and said that they were coming over with Grandma West if it got closer. A few minutes later, Beverly Young (Beckham) called to see if Bradd, Dawn and the girls could come over. I told her she better come to, but she declined.

Now the TV is saying that the tornado is moving straight north on Hwy. 183. I turned on the scanner and they are saying that a house has been hit. Here comes Bruce Foster into the house; followed by my parents, grandma, and Bradd with his family.

It was not much longer when the sirens started going off. This was not good. For some reason, I knew that things were going to get bad. I told everybody to go on down stairs and wait, just in case.

Bradd and I decided to stand out on the front porch and watch the lightning flash. We could see Carl Wingfield in his apartment, kicked back in his recliner and watching TV. I finally told Bradd that I would feel bad if that old man got killed and that I was going to go get him. When I got to his door, I looked at his TV to see what was so interesting that kept him in his chair. I guessed wrong on what he might have been watching. It was not, "Girls Gone Wild." I cannot remember what he was watching, but it was not justifying him staying in that chair. With little persuasion, Carl went with me to the house.

A couple of minutes later, I called Susan to see if she could remember where marker sixty-one was at. She said no and asked me why. I told her that the guy said on the scanner that it was a huge tornado. She then thought it was close to the 183/54 Hwy. junction. I said, "I love you!" and hung up.

Bradd and I were on the porch again when the hail and wind got really bad. Bradd thought that we should go downstairs right now. As soon as we got inside the house, the lights went out and the

Jason West House Before

Photo by Ken and Mary Jean West

siren quit. That was an eerie feeling. We were not in the basement ten seconds when debris started hitting the house. I could see dust reflecting off the flashlight. I started smelling old lumber and cedar trees. Then my ears started to feel the pressure and I immediately knew it was hitting the house.

There were eleven of us under a queen-sized mattress in the kids playroom. We could hear the roof go. Then it got really loud. To me, it sounded like all the windows in your vehicle are down and all you hear is the wind swirling around in your ears as you drive as fast as you can.

I never thought that we were going to die, but I was getting concerned. I knew that it was on top of us for awhile but I didn't know how long. When it was over, I looked up and I could see that the floor above was still there. I knew we were all ok. So, I walked up the stairs and opened the door to HELL. I could see our roof was gone. My folk's van was against the walkway into the garage. The water tower was gone. My grandma's house was destroyed. Arnie and Roberta Schmidt's house was leveled. My pickup was mangled. Right where Carl was sitting in his chair was a pile of rubble. I could see that the whole town was gone! When I looked back to the south, I could see skeletons of trees and houses. Due to everybody being in shock, nobody could believe me. I called Susan on the cell phone. All I could get out to her before the phone went dead was that our house was gone, it's all gone and we were ok.

Bradd could hear someone calling for help. He headed for Arnie's house while I headed for my pickup to get a flashlight. Bradd yelled at me to hurry up and get over to him. He found Roberta and she was hurt really bad. When I got there, she was lying on her stomach. There was no debris around her. I told her who we were as she continued to holler for help. We could see that she was bleeding from her head. I handed him a blanket that just happened to be next to me and told him to stop the bleeding. Bradd asked, "How am I going to do that?" I said, "You were a Boy Scout and don't suffocate her!" Bradd did an excellent job! I then heard my neighbor, Bill

Moss, saying he could hear Arnie hollering from a pile of debris. I hurried over to Bill and told Arnie I was there. Calvin Donohue and girlfriend's son showed up the same time I got to Bill. Since I couldn't find my flashlight and the lightning was not as persistent as it once was, Calvin had his penlight which worked quite well.

We finally got Arnie found and pulled the debris off and away from him. Calvin and Bill had to convince him that I was capable of carrying him out of the rubble. I carried Arnie to his driveway and told him that Roberta was hurt. We could see Bradd, Bruce Foster, my dad, Ken, and Brandon Hosheit with her. I truly believed that she was not going to make it. Just then a fire truck or ambulance pulled up. Bradd, Calvin and his girlfriend's son, and I headed across the street to check on Bryan Foster's house. Bill thought he could hear someone, but we could not. So, Bill went back to his house to check on Bev and others on the way. When we got to Bev's house, we found her alright. Her house was still there and that her vehicle and Buddy's pickup were ok and operational. We took Buddy's pickup to Apache Services to get flashlights and Calvin's pickup.

Bradd and I went and checked out his house. It suffered severely. Then we went back to my house. I found my two German Shorthair dogs alive! I could not believe it. Everybody was gone. So we went to my folk's and found dad there a short time later. His house had severe damage as well. We got his pickup out from under the neighbors huge Pine tree. We went our separate ways again. Before dad left, he said everybody was going to Haviland and to go to Dillon's to let them know we were alive.

Every once in a while, the cell phone would ring and either it was Susan, Buddy, or other friends trying to make sure we were alright. The only place the cell phones worked was at Apache Services.

As we made our way around, we checked on Merle Collins place and found him trying to get his garage door off one of his cars. So, we got that done for him. He told us that he and his family went for a "hell of a ride," and he was off to Pratt.

Bradd and I made it back to Bev's house and found Buddy, from

Jason West House After

Photo by Ken and Mary Jean West

Harper, with his mom. Buddy had borrowed his stepdad's pickup to drive because his was acting up. It never acted up on us! We all decided to stay at Bev's house until morning. A short time later, a state trooper came and told us it was a mandatory evacuation and we needed to go. So, we loaded up "the one-legged, crippled old lady" into her vehicle and off to Haviland we went.

That night was a night we will all remember. From the devastation, to the tragedy, and to the heroism that everyone experienced, I am grateful that my wife and kids did not have go through the tornado itself. The aftermath was an experience all of its own.

I would like to thank everyone who helped my family and I. Thank you is necessary to say to SemCrude, Red Cross, Salvation Army (my extra change will always find your red kettle) Audie and Amanda McFarlen, and our friends in Hays who brought us clothes and essentials, which they purchased with money they rounded up at the wedding we were supposed to attend on May 5. Also thank you is given to everyone else who helped in some small way.

We decided to stay and build back where we were in Greensburg before the storm. Things will be different for awhile. It is just something we all have to get use to.

submitted by: MARY LINENBROKER
OLD ADDRESS: 223 N. GROVE • GREENSBURG, KS 67054
NEW ADDRESS: 605 S. BAY • GREENSBURG, KS 67054

God Bless Greensburg

I spent the day doing usual things around the house. I had a supper engagement with Don Richard; he was going to cook. QT Pie and I drove over to Don's. He was happy to see us. The evening went as usual. We ate, did dishes and then went in the living room to watch TV.

The weather came up on the bottom of TV set—storm warnings around Protection. Well, we had those warnings the week before; nothing happened. Then, they said it looked like the town of Greensburg would be in the path of the tornado. It looked ok outside at that time. However, I said to Don, "I guess I'll go home." He said, "Where will you go?" I said, "Oh, I'll take QT Pie and get in my closet."

I drove home, put the car away, and went into the house. I turned on the TV. The cable TV said the tornado was coming directly to Greensburg and everyone to take cover. By that time, the siren was blowing. I went to the bathroom, got my medication and put it in a plastic sack. I picked up a big flashlight and my purse. I put on my rain coat, got my Red Hat blanket and QT Pie, my dog. We went in the closet. I had a container full of winter clothes. I pushed the hangers to the east and the rest to the west and made room on floor for my feet. I sat on the container and put the blanket over my back and head. I held my purse and plastic bag in one hand and my light in the other. My briefcase was beside the container on the floor. When the tornado started, it sounded like hail hitting the roof. Then, the electricity went off and I turned on the lantern so we wouldn't be in the dark. I shut the closet door and held onto the door knob. By that time, it was full blown. All the noise you can ever think of were happening: windows breaking, wood splintering, walls falling, roof blowing away, trees torn to shreds, highline wire popping and the wind whirling like a jet engine. When the roof left, part of something fell on my arm and QT Pie. She howled and climbed up as far as she could on my shoulders. I cried and thought I might die. Things were hitting the house. It was so loud and wet with the rain pouring in. The wind quit and I thought it was over. But, it started again with more rain and more things hitting the house. Then, it was gone.

QT Pie and I pushed against the closet door and did get it open

enough to get out of the closet. I had to leave the briefcase in the closet. I put over my left arm the plastic sack, my purse and QT Pie. I held the flashlight in my right hand. I looked around the bedroom. The air conditioner was in the hallway door. The wall was leaning and pushing my dresser to a degree that the drawers were open and full of water. There was lath and plaster everywhere. The bed was overturned. The windows were gone as well as the side of the house. We crawled going over the AC and debris in hall. All of Ralph's cars were on the floor with broken glass. We made it to the living room. Chairs were in piles. The window was broke out and curtains gone or out the window. I couldn't get out the front door. The front of the house had collapsed on to itself. I worked my way into the kitchen. It looked pretty good by flashlight, except for no roof. We went on into the laundry room. I sat QT Pie on the dryer and found a towel in her basket and dried her off best I could. It was still raining. I went to the back door. There was no roof but the door wouldn't open. The window was gone but the steel bars Ralph put on them were in place; I couldn't get out.

My neighbors across the street were in the street calling to anyone needing help. I flashed my flashlight and called out to Jerry that I couldn't get out. He came crawling over about four feet of tangled debris and tried to open the door. It was wedged shut. He left and returned with three men who forced the door open. They helped QT Pie and me over the debris to the street. My neighbors were there and all wet. Mr. Goodman's car had broken windows and was dented but was running. He put me in the front seat. Frances Noland was in the back seat lying down. She had a hurt hand and was bleeding. He took us up to Highway 54. I got out as I was not hurt. There was already police, ambulances, and the Red Cross helping everyone. I sat on a tree log that had fallen. My neighbor, Phyllis Brown, and her daughter, Carol, and their dog were sitting there.

Some one made the announcement to the crowd that everyone was to go to the KDOT building and register. Then they said, "Anyone need a ride?" I said yes. I got a ride with a man and some students that were on their way to Salina for a meeting and came in on the end of the tornado. The students sat on their luggage in the back of the van. He took five or six of us. There we registered. Then some one said, "Haviland High School Gym is open and the Red Cross has cots for you. Who would like to go?" I put my hand up and got in another van and was taken to Haviland. We registered again and I got to go inside. I was cold and wet. My cell phone wouldn't work. One young man (I think a student at the Haviland College) said come outside and we'll try to reach a phone number for you. By that time, it was 1:30 a.m. He talked to Chris and told my daughter, Melanie, where I was. By that time, TV had pictures of the devastation of Greensburg. I went back in the building and because of QT Pie, I didn't get a cot. It was around 2:30 a.m. when someone said I could have a cot. They gave my dog a drink of water and dog food. They asked if I needed to call someone. I needed to call David, my son, in Colorado. So, they got me in line to use a regular phone for three minutes. I got to talk to David and Becky around 3:00 a.m. My ex-daughter-in-law, Ada, had called David and told him Greensburg was hit hard. Then I went back to my cot.

Someone brought a trash bag of socks. I went over and found a pair. I was so glad to get warm socks. I covered QT Pie up with a blanket and I laid down and tried to get warm. Around 7:00 a.m., a friend, Candy, came by and brought me some hot coffee. I saw a lot of people from Haviland come to help us. I saw my neighbors crying; no one had anything left. It was so sad. I was so happy to see my Melanie and Chris come through that gym door. It was about 11:30 a.m.

No one could go back into Greensburg. We went around the north side of town and tried to see what had happened. All you could see were trees stripped of leaves and branches and all the buildings flattened in heaps. We had a room in a Kinsley Motel due to the calling around from Sandy Shepherd (Colleyville, TX). Thank you so much. David came with his big truck to help find belongings and haul them

to storage units. Deetz Shepherd helped load and pack up anything that was usable. Deetz was with a church group from Colleyville, TX.

God bless all that were here to help us. I know the Lord was with me as I was not hurt; one small bruise on my arm. The closet proved to be the best place in the demolished house.

4-4-08 Time has gone on. I am now in my new home. Thanks be to God! I was home sick for my home and people I knew. So I bought a pre-built house from a contractor; we had our differences and had the family do most of the talking. My concrete cracked on my porch; very disappointing and needed changed. I had a round with the tax people at the courthouse that set me back a step or two. It didn't make sense paying taxes on two houses. I know now an old lady like myself should not jump in and build a house. I didn't know one stick from another. I miss my old home and my dog, QT Pie who died on September 24, 2007. I have received so much help and been given so many gifts. I can't name all the people who helped and gave of their money, but thanks to my family, Melanie and Chris Fredrickson, his sister, Sandy, and husband, Deetz, David and Becky Linenbroker and to Don Richard's family that helped me move to my new home. Thanks for all your prayers then and now and in the future. I have been so blessed with a new lot to build on, new house, some old and some new furniture, new dishes, pots and pans, appliances, big yard that needs lot of landscaping, new storm shelter, some old and new clothes and new shoes too! I lost a lot of stuff and I enjoyed my stuff because I like to craft. I have to humbly thank the Lord that saved me that night. I was not hurt but I felt my life was over. I have had some hard days.

I have a part-time job at The Big Well in Greensburg. I get to see people and visit with them. Life is better each day. I am so lucky to be here. I am better off today than I was before the EF-5 tornado that took away my home and town. God bless the volunteers and God bless Greensburg, KS!

New House of Mary Linenbroker   *Photo by Mary Linenbroker*

submitted by: **MARION AND ELLA MAE MARRS**
OLD ADDRESS: 421 W. WISCONSIN • GREENSBURG, KS 67054
NEW ADDESS: 522 W. IOWA AVE. • GREENSBURG, KS 67054

It Was a Nightmare

May 4, 2007 — Marion and I were attending the Spring Kansas State Good Sam Jamboree in Hutchinson, Kansas. Around 9:15 p.m. after an evening program, we went back to our motor home and turned on our TV to learn that there was a big storm headed for Greensburg. The TV station, that we were watching, was talking to a storm chaser on his cell phone that was on Highway 183 following the tornado into Greensburg. We could see by his pictures he was taking by the lightning flashes that the tornado was very large and headed straight for our home town. Soon, the storm spotter was helping families along 183 out of their homes that had been hit by the storm. As he came into town, you could see all the damage the EF-5 tornado had done. He then went to the Dillon's parking lot and talked to the survivors. It was a nightmare! We sat and watched the tornado, until 3:30 a.m., go all the way to the Nebraska border on radar.

Early Saturday morning, we left Hutchinson for Greensburg. We only got as far as the Evergreen RV Park in Pratt. This is where we parked the RV until August 12. On Monday morning, we sat in line about three miles east of Greensburg before we could get back into town. What a sight we encountered when we drove up to our home. The house was still standing but the windows were all blown out as well as the doors, the roof had raised and came back down over the family room on the south, the west wall was leaning outward and everything was soaked from the rain and hail. The basement was intact except for a ten foot beam through the new windows we had put in along with a new $15,000.00 wall in 2005. Also, a 9x18 inch board was through the basement door.

We salvaged clothes and personal things but lost most of the living room furniture, kitchen and all the family room furniture because of the rain. We built a new garage at 522 W. Iowa in June 2007 and brought our things from storage from Pratt. Marion and I left for South Texas on September 30, 2007 for five and a half months as we didn't want to spend the winter in our motor home here. We have been living in our motor home while we are building our new home at 522 W. Iowa Avenue. I lived at this address for fifty years with my late husband, Leon Deckert, who passed away on February 20, 2001.

Marion and Ella Mae Marrs House Before   *Photo by Ella Mae Marrs*

Besides losing the two properties, we lost a rental at 419 W. Morton.

So many people and organizations have been so good to us with their help and prayers. We have been on TV several times and have heard from friends and family all over the United States that had seen us on national TV. A friend from California sent an article where

Marion was featured riding his lawnmower cutting weeds at 421 W. Wisconsin in July, 2007. We were also featured on Hatteburg People on channel 10 in May, 2007 and again May 4, 2008 in a follow up story before we started building our house. We plan to have our home mostly done before we leave for South Texas for the winter.

Marion and Ella Mae Marrs House After   *Photo by Ella Mae Marrs*

submitted by: **JERRY AND HELEN KOEHN**
OLD ADDRESS: 416 S. SPRUCE • GREENSBURG, KS 67054
NEW ADDRESS: 100 E. GRANT • GREENSBURG, KS 67054

Our Lives Have Forever Changed

May 4, 2007 — The date we will never forget. A typical Friday — We usually go to the lake on Friday afternoon, but we were having a garage sale Saturday morning. So, we weren't going till after that. Otherwise, we wouldn't have been at home Friday night! We had been watching the TV and the sirens started going off; usually when that happens we don't pay any attention or we go out to see what's going on! But not this time! Jeff's wife, Karin, was visiting her brother so he came to our house with his dog, Max, about 9:20 p.m. or so. We went to the basement with our dog, Breezy, and got in the southwest room under a table, covered up with pillows and waited until the tornadoes (three of them) were over. We thought we might be trapped in the basement but we were able to get up the stairs and out. Jerry and I stayed in the basement all night.

Jeff went out and walked around to see if he could help anyone. He came back in the middle of the night. He said he had to stop

sometimes and figure out where he was. I told him how can you get lost in Greensburg; you have lived here all your life! We were told the next morning we had to evacuate the town and we went outside and saw the damage. I began to understand how you could not know where you were. It was devastating!

We were taken to Dillon's parking lot to board a bus that took us to Mullinville to the shelter at the school. We were sitting there with our dogs and they came and told us "no pets" in the shelter. Guess we were going to the street! HA! Jessica Clayton came over and told us we could go to her mom's house, Ron and Susan Clayton. Having dogs was not a problem; she had a kennel. She took us there and we stayed with them for a week. They took wonderful care of us. They cooked us breakfast every morning before we left to go to Greensburg. I don't know what we would have done without them. They are special to us.

They let us go back into Greensburg on Monday morning. Oh my, what a shock! There was so much destruction; debris everywhere. We drove down our street to our house which was still standing with four walls and the roof. It was moved off the foundation about a foot. The north wall in the living room was hanging out from the house, you could see the ground. That wall had no sheet rock or insulation on it. It was the only one that way in the whole house.

We worked there everyday for a week, cleaning up, salvaging what we could. It was awful. Then we had to find someplace to store everything. We wound up with a storage place in Medicine Lodge and at our friends house there.

Don't know what we would have done if it hadn't been for our dear friends from Medicine Lodge, Jerry's sister, all of her family and everyone else that helped.

Not only did we lose our house, but also my mom's house, where Jeff and Karin lived. The house I grew up in!

Mike and Lisa lost their house too. They were on the north end of town where the damage wasn't so bad in some places. We saved our big shed, it was damaged, but it was still in good shape. We have since had it repaired.

Our camper was parked at the Coldwater Lake, so we had a place to go. We lived there for two months. I always wanted to do that, not any more!

We lived in Mullinville in a rental house for a year. We moved back to Greensburg on July 1, 2008 in Prairie Pointe on Main Street where the school was; actually we are where the art room was located! It is so good being back "home" in Greensburg! How our lives have forever changed!

submitted by: **CARL AND JOAN HAYSE**
603 S. MAPLE • GREENSBURG, KS 67054

Construction

Recalling the night of May 4th, is like reliving a nightmare, but it's over and we're thankful to be alive. We walked away from our damaged home that night with our daughter-in-law, Monica and grandson, Darren. Our first thought was that our area of town was the only one hit, but we soon learned the full extent of the damage and the fact that we were on the edge of the storm and worst demolition was near the center of town. As we walked out in pitch black night with only flashlights to guide us, we became aware of the complete devastation. We walked by neighbor's houses lying in the street, by the school where brick walls were lowered to a few feet, and down main street strewn with tree branches, rubble,

Carl and Joan Hayse House Before

Photo by Joan Hayse

50

and electric lines. As we continued toward the business district, we met people looking for relatives and the brick two-story businesses were unrecognizable, completely down; only piles of brick remained. Police cars were picking people up, driving with flat tires that were punctured by nail-filled boards in the street. We continued on seeing cars overturned, horns and buzzers sounding, lights on with doors open; some having landed in the buildings, on trees, rolled like tin cans. We saw the old Methodist Church completely down.

We finally made it back to Bay Street where Monica and Darren had been forced to park as that was as far as they could drive with roads blocked. They parked behind a semi-trailer turned over on the highway. We drove back to Dale and Monica's house where we stayed that night and for 2 ½ months. During that time, we cleaned out our house and stored the contents in a building in Mullinville. Dale, Darol, Dean, and their two boys helped us tremendously in this endeavor; as did Paul and Mike Hayse who came from Pratt to help us move.

After our belongings were cleaned out of the house, we started clearing the lot where our business, Hayse Greenhouse and Garden Center, was located. The Garden Center building was badly damaged. The old blacksmith shop, which served as our storage building, was a pile of crumbled brick and of course, all of the greenhouses were destroyed; vanished.

We were blessed with help from family at this time. My sister, Gerry Yock, came from Amarillo on Mother's Day weekend to give moral support and she helped clean out the water soaked Garden Center. Heavy rains had soaked what didn't blow away. Another sister, Marci Simmons, came from Phoenix to help; what a lifesaver she was. My sister, Vada, and her husband, John Quick, came from Hutchinson and helped sort greenhouse merchandise.

Our garage and house at 603 S. Maple had to be bulldozed and removed. All we have now are two big elm trees, a basement foundation, a fish pond, and a slab where our garage and shop were located. Fifty-four years of blood, sweat, and tears have been taken away, but we're okay.

Four months after the horrific event, we are survivors looking to the future. We are now residents of the FEMA village. This mobile home park is located just south of the Greensburg city limits. Prior to the tornado, this area was to be a new housing development. Two new model homes had been built and they were also destroyed. We have about 300 FEMA trailers in this park; occupied by over 450 people. We have close neighbors; only about fifteen feet separates our trailers. Our streets are paved and we have access to cable or dish TV, telephone lines, and electricity. As in most towns, we have trash collection and street lights at each corner. We receive mail using our old addresses at a post office box located outside the temporary (modular building) Post Office in Greensburg. Our FEMA home is a three-bedroom trailer with living/dining area and kitchen. Our bath is quite large and washer/dryer are located in the hallway. The air conditioner works well and we are very comfortable. The trailer was presented to us complete with stove, refrigerator, microwave, coffee pot, dishes and silverware, beds and bedding, towels, sofa, chair, coffee and end tables, and a dining table and chairs. We only needed clothes and food when we moved in.

Although Carl says that starting over at 86 was not in our plans, we're okay because of all the support through love, prayers, gifts of labor, money, clothes, etc. from Red Cross, Salvation Army, numerous religious organizations, fire departments, police departments, National Guard, and caring individuals including our family and friends. Kind words of encouragement and love helped us in this recovery period. We can never thank people enough for all the things they did for us.

Many new homes have been built and more are in various stages of construction. Our home is being built on our lot at 603 S. Maple. That was our site of our home for 54 years. We hope to move in by the Spring of 2009. We are now officially retired. May 4, 2007 finalized that decision in our lives. The storm has given us a deeper appreciation for what we have and confirmed to us the saying, "The best things in life are not things." God willing, we will have a home in the thriving town of Greensburg again.

Carl and Joan Hayse House Before

Photo by Joan Hayse

submitted by: LEROY AND CHARLOTTE KRAFT

115 W. GARFIELD • GREENSBURG, KS 67054

14206 E. WATSON • WICHTIA, KS 67230

Miss Our Neighbors And Friends

I have put off writing "my story" for about a year. I felt it was time to put it down, for my grandchildren and their children, so they know what Grandpa Leroy and Grandma Charlotte went through during that time on May 4, 2007.

The week prior to May 4, Leroy and I finished painting the Daylight Donut building. The last thing we did was Leroy painted the awning and we talked about getting the floor tiles replaced. We were to be on our way to Olathe on Saturday to hear our grandson, Jackson, age 5, to play his first piano concert. We were so looking forward to hearing him play, as he is very gifted.

On Friday, May 4th, Leroy commented that maybe he should stay and finish getting the floor in the Donut Shop ready for replacement. We decided that could wait and we would go Saturday morning for Olathe. After lunch on the 4th, we thought that we could just leave today and stay with Mike and Christine in Andover and have a chance to visit a very dear friend of ours, Mama Louise, who was in the hospital in Wichita. So, we left a day early. By the time we completed visiting and was getting ready for bed, Christine informed us that she tuned into the weather and exclaimed, "Mom and Dad, I think you need to see this!" We watched and listened and not a sound was heard from any of us. We were stunned.

After realizing what was actually happening, we looked at each other and silently put our shoes back on and left to return to Greensburg to see the extent of the damage.

While driving in complete silence, except for the radio, I kept thinking that it can't be as bad as the media was reporting. They always over exaggerate everything … telling myself … we will get there and check on neighbors, get our house settled and let the kids know everything was OK.

While this was going on in my mind, I knew what Leroy was thinking, he is the more analytical one. Of course, not saying a word … we drove on. I got out my rosary and began praying one Hail Mary at a time, with each Hail Mary, I would focus on each neighbor, each friend, and finally on each person in Greensburg who might need help in anyway. I just prayed everyone was OK.

While driving closer to Greensburg, we saw emergency and medical vehicles; one after another coming from and going to that direction. My heart was beating so fast, I had to stop and breathe, for I had literally stopped breathing.

We got as far as the outskirts of town and police turned us around. They were still trying to contain the area and also looking for any fatalities. They feared the deaths would reach a high toll. Leroy decided we would take a back road to town and off we went. We did not get very far, when we came across a huge tree (all of it, roots and all) lying in the middle of the road. Since there was no way around it, we turned around and headed back to Pratt to look for a room for the night. To my total amazement, there was no place to go. I could not believe that aid had come so quickly. We decided to sleep in our SUV in the Walmart vacant parking lot. No, neither one of us slept,

as we were just realizing that this was as bad as it had been reported and we were shocked, once again.

The next morning we headed back to Greensburg only to be turned away once again. At that point, we still couldn't see into town and visualize the damage that had been done. So, we headed back to Haviland to check on neighbors and friends.

When we got there, I was searching for Bill and Shelby Waymire and just cried when at last I found them to be safe. From then on, it was one after the other, found safe! I felt so much better. Later, we find out that a good friend, Beverly Volz, did not make it. I was very sad and knew I would miss her. She was only one of eleven who did not survive this terrible event of nature. They will all be missed.

We were on the phone constantly with our kids. Diane, Christine and Amy and husbands were close enough to be there when we needed the support. Our concern were the boys who needed to come and see the devastation; not only to their home but to their school and town. Adam, being on the Police Force in Florida, was pulling all kinds of strings to get back in time to help clean up our lot. John, in California and at the end of the school term, was very doubtful he could make it in time. At that time, we thought we had only three days to clear out. On Sunday evening, John called and said his lab students and his advisor pitched in and gave him a ticket to "go home and be with your family". Yeah, I cried at the news. So, Eric picked up Adam in Kansas City and then they picked up John in Wichita and drove out to Greensburg; only to find all the sources for good memories gone. Each one of our children took this very hard to see all the destruction. They especially took it hard to the house their dad literally built and rebuilt with his own hands and skill. Leroy had just completed remodeling the entire house and we were working on the outside. He built his "Serenity Now" part of the yard on the west side and was now planning on a deck in the middle of the yard. There wouldn't be a "Serenity", no more deck plans; only plans as what to do next!

We spent a month with Amy and Paul and the girls and then a month in an apartment in Wichita. Only then, did we finally decide to find a house in Wichita and start over. Christine and Mike and family are about one mile away. Amy and Paul and girls are about thirty minutes to Newton. Diane and Howard and family are about one hour to Salina. Eric and Jenn and family are about three hours to Olathe. Adam and Julie and family and John fly in and are so easy to pick them up and continue our family-get-togethers. That is all good.

So, we are here and Leroy is finishing the basement. We are gaining ground every day. We still miss our neighbors and friends that we saw everyday going and coming to work, walking to the theater, walking to church and just plain walking anywhere we wanted. But, it is good here and we will soon have good memories here too. God watched over us then and he will watch over us now and forever.

I found this note from one of our grandchildren after that terrible weekend. This sums it up for all of them.

"Things that are gone: a painting by me and Elizabeth, when we were very young; two by MOM; Hunter Drug Store; the ancient theatre; all of Main Street; Grandpa's "Serenity Now"; the Big Well Museum; Christmas decorations; little wooden figures with our names; dozens of pictures; a house of memories. All in all, they're just things … but they all had a special place in my heart. Now, it's thrown across the county in millions of pieces. And now I have to deal with it."

submitted by: **KENNY AND PEGGY BANTA**
OLD ADDRESS: 515 W. KANSAS • GREENSBURG, KS 67054
NEW ADDRESS: 306 E. IOWA • GREENSBURG, KS 67054

Get to The Basement

My husband, Kenny, and I were managers of the Best Western J-Hawk Motel when the tornado struck Greensburg. On the night of the tornado, we were in Garden City, Kansas helping set up for the Kansas Sampler Festival. Our youngest son, Jerry Diemart, was in charge of the motel that weekend. He called us about 9:40 p.m. and told us a tornado was about to hit Greensburg. I immediately said, "Hang up and get to the basement!" Before I could get that whole sentence out, we got cut off. Erica Goodman, Karen Martin and us immediately went to our room at the motel and turned the TV on only to hear that the tornado had struck. They were afraid about sixty-seven percent of Greensburg was destroyed. We were all horrified and were going to leave to go back to Greensburg immediately. But, I decided to call the Highway Patrol first. They said we were not to go anywhere because there were power lines down all over. They had all the roads closed and we would not be let in. So, we kept the TV on and tried to get what rest we could.

About 3:00 a.m., Erica called us and said her husband was at the Pratt Hospital; his injuries had been treated and he could leave the hospital. We all decided to go to Pratt, bypassing Greensburg. We picked up Gary and went on to Haviland. In the meantime, some emergency workers had a mobile phone and Jerry called us to tell us that the Banta family was all okay. Jerry, our oldest son, Mick, and grandson, Corey, had helped the emergency workers the rest of the night look for survivors and help them get to the Dillon's parking lot and from there transferred to Mullinville and Haviland. When we got to Haviland and got out of our car, some workers that had been staying at the motel came running up to tell us that our boys were alright because they had just seen them. We thought that was really thoughtful of them because until we saw them we really couldn't believe that they were still in one piece. Luckily, we had a very small two bedroom trailer on our farm north of Greensburg that was still standing. We had no electricity, but a roof over our head to keep us out of the rain. The next day we were able to retrieve our generator and have some electricity.

When the law enforcement officers let us back into Greensburg, we were horrified at what we found. The TV did not even do the damage justice. The motel was totaled. We were, however, able to save a few of our treasures; mainly what we had in the basement. My husband had just finished his new 35'x40' foot shed. He had just moved all his tools, saws, Model T's and treasures in. It was totally destroyed and almost everything in it was gone except one Model T that was badly damaged and parts of the other one that he was ready to put together.

We lived in the trailer for the next three or four months until we were able to get into Clair's little rent house that had not been totally destroyed, but badly damaged. We are still living in that house; still trying to get organized.

submitted by: **KENNETH WEST**
327 S. ELM DRIVE • GREENSBURG, KS 67054

Our Town Has Changed

I guess you could say my luck has not been good over the last few years. First, I lost my major retirement funds when Enron went bankrupt. Then Mother Nature took a shot at me and now my house is gone with the wind. I almost wish my house had burned to the ground so I wouldn't have had to sort throughout the memories that were left scattered around. It was really hard to decide what to try to save and what to give up on.

My town that I grew up in — the schools that I went to, the old-time theater, Hunter's Drug store with its old-time soda fountain where you could get a cold Coke and sit on a tall bar stool and turn circles, the city swimming pool where I spent my summers as a child — has all changed forever. In general, my old town only exists in my memory and that of others.

The day of May 4, 2007 was like most other days. I had gotten off work at 6:00 a.m. and had slept a few hours before going outside to mow. I was to have the weekend off before working the next week on the day shift.

I can't remember the exact time but my wife, Mary Jean, and I had been watching storm reports on TV coming out of Oklahoma on and off for about an hour. The weather reports were showing tornado activity around Ashland and Protection, Kansas and heading towards Kiowa County.

We called my mom, Ruth West, and told her we would pick her up and go to my son's, Jason West, basement. She told us that she would just stay home and go to her closet if things got bad. We told her that she needed to go with us and that we were coming to get her.

After getting to Jason's, we put our van in his garage to protect it from hail. That didn't work out too well as we found out later. Before we arrived, Jason had gone to Carl Wingfield's apartment next door to tell Carl he needed to get over to his basement. Carl is an elderly man who really didn't want to go. Jason told Carl that he could walk over to his house or he would carry him over there, but he was going with him now no matter what. Carl decided he would walk over with Jason. It was a good thing as Carl's apartment disappeared with the tornado.

So, we had Carl Wingfield, Ruth West, Dawn and Bradd Beckham and their two young daughters, Janie and Heidi, Bruce Foster, Jason West, Mary Jean West and myself, Kenneth West in the basement along with Jason's family pet, a small dog named Sadie. Jason's wife, Susan, and their children, Tierra, Bo and Brett, had left about one and a half hours earlier to go visit Susan's mother and step-dad, Alice and Tony Boor, near Larned.

So, now you have ten people and one small dog in a basement with a tornado bearing down on a small town. A tornado changing our lives in twenty minutes and our small town Main Street U.S.A. forever.

Kenneth and Mary Jean West House Before   *Photo by Kenneth and Mary Jean West*

The noise of the storm was picking up and the sirens were going full blast. Jason and I were holding a queen size mattress in front of and over ten people and one dog crowded into a corner of a basement room — with everyone on the box springs of the bed. The basement windows blew in as the tornado hit, sending flying glass through the room, some of which was embedded in the mattress, and cut my hand slightly on the side holding the mattress. Then, the full brunt of the front side of the tornado hit. You could hear my son's house starting to crumble and blow away. The pressure change was heavy and I couldn't think of anything except to hang on to the mattress. The best way I can describe the pressure changes is to tell you to pinch your nose shut, close your mouth, and blow; forcing air into your ears as hard as you can. Release and then do it again as the back side of the tornado hits. Release and then wait for the ringing to stop; in about two weeks. The back side of the tornado hit and we could hear the roof and the walls of the house leave with a crumbling roar. Then it was almost calm except for the fading rumble going away from our location. We checked everyone for injuries and there were non except for my right hand with the minor glass cut.

A little later, after we were sure everything was clear, Jason, Bruce, Bradd and I went up the stairs to check things out. We had to exit over what was left of my mini-van. The only light other than the flashlights we had was the emergency flashers going on and off on our van and the Beckham's van. They had parked theirs in the street curbside but it ended up on its side beside the front of Jason's house. Cell phones were not working very well, if at all. You had just seconds to text or say words like "alive" or "okay".

Jason, Bradd and I went over to Arnie and Roberta Schmidt's house to check on them. Jason and Bradd dug Arnie out and put him on a clear spot wrapped in a blanket. Jason carried Arnie to the street. Roberta was badly injured. I located an emergency vehicle or ambulance coming up the street and directed them to Jason, who was with Roberta in the rubble of her home.

Carl's granddaughter, Mandy Green from Sawyer, arrived to get Carl. After they left, I started walking towards my house to see if I had somewhere to take my mom and wife that was intact and dry. My house was about four and a half blocks away. I was working my way through the debris in the streets. A war zone would have looked better. I broke down six to eight house doors to let people out after hearing them call out for help. There were no injuries to the people I let out. I could not recognize where I was at and can't remember who they were. I guess you could call it a form of shock.

I found Bay Street and could only recognize it by its width. I was within a block of my house and saw a flashlight blinking where Jim Bettes' trailer house was. Mr. Bettes was under chunks of what was left of his trailer. I pulled pieces off him and got him set up against a piece of the trailer. I saw Chris Wirth's pickup coming toward me. I waved him down and had him stay with Jim. I left to get an EMT crew down the street to them.

I arrived at my house. The roof was off and the south and west bedroom walls were blown out. Giving up on my house as a place of refuge, I headed back to Jason's house by a different route. I went through water two to three feet deep in places and over downed power lines that I hoped weren't live. I think the water came from the water tower when it came down at the Big Well Park.

I got back to Jason's house and found a couple and their dog in a small car that had come to the hospital to help. (They were Shane and Kim Stephenson of Olathe, KS who were on their way to visit relatives in Ford, KS. They had just happened to be nearing Greensburg shortly after the tornado. They also had medical and emergency training so were allowed into town to help.) I asked if they could get my mom, wife and the two little Beckham girls out to the KDOT building on the east edge of town where I had heard they were gathering people to eventually bus to the Haviland School Gym. They willingly did so.

Jason, Bradd, and Bruce left to check other houses in the area.

Kenneth and Mary Jean West House After
Photo by Kenneth and Mary Jean West

Dawn and I walked across town to the east side to check on Beverly Young, Bradd's mother and our close friend. Bev is in a wheelchair due to having had her foot amputated in November 2005. She's a diabetic. The way to Bev's house looked like a refugee walk with people headed to the KDOT building. Bev's house was standing but was damaged. She was okay and refused to go with us. One of her sons, Buddy, was already with her as he had driven from his home in Harper, KS (about one and a half hours away) as soon as he heard the tornado had destroyed Greensburg.

We got to the KDOT building and it was chock full of people. I found Mary Jean and mom and stayed with them until they were headed out of town on a large bus for Haviland. Dawn and her daughters left on the bus, too. I stayed in town to check on other friends and property. I got to Randy and Nancy Reed's house and they were okay. The house was slightly damaged but dry so they had taken in approximately a dozen or so people. I then left and worked my way back across town to my house to see if I could get my pickup out from under a large pine tree so I could have transportation. After checking my pickup, Jason and Buddy Beckham showed up in Buddy's pickup to help me lift some tree limbs so I could move my pickup. I got my pickup started, put it in gear, and gunned it out

from under the tree. Surprisingly, it was in pretty good shape except for a cracked windshield, dings, dents and a bed load of tornado trash. I picked my way through streets back to Randy and Nancy's house. Jason and Buddy went to Bev's. Rather than risk waking people up at Reed's, I spent the rest of the night in my pickup. At least it was full of gas. I dried myself out by running the heater in the pickup then nodded off for a couple of hours.

At first light, I worked my pickup out of town and headed for Haviland. When I got close to Haviland, my cell phone had a couple of bars of connection showing. So, I called Jan West, my sister-in-law, on her cell phone and told her where my mom was supposed to be. The country home of my brother, Gene, and Jan was okay. (It's the same home my mom was born and raised in.) Jan and I arrived at the Haviland Gym within minutes of each other. Mom left to go home with Jan. Mary Jean and I went to Pratt to her sister, Linda Brehm's house. After getting to Pratt, we went to Walmart first to buy underwear and makeup, the necessities of life!!

This is my story of the night of the tornado and part of the day after. Our lives have changed, our town has changed, and we will have to adjust ourselves to memories we have and to keepsakes and things we have lost.

Bruce Fosters Garage   *Photo by Bruce Foster*

submitted by: LANA KEPHART
DAUGHTER OF MELVIN AND LENA SIMMONS
THEIR OLD ADDRESS: 407 S. GROVE • GREENSBURG, KS 67054

Greensburg is Rebuilding

I had been keeping in phone contact with my sisters about the potential severe weather heading towards Greensburg. Diane, who lives outside of Buffalo, Oklahoma with her husband, Mike, and daughter, Tori, said they had "dodged the bullet" down there and we were all likely to get it. Kandi, who lives in Medicine Lodge with her family, was keeping an eye on the radar on Channel 12 and I was watching Channel 3 from my home in Hoisington. We were getting more concerned by the minute. And, when the storm chasers came on the air and were describing this monster cell, destroying the Mennonite community outside of Greensburg, we knew this was a bad deal. I called the folks to make sure they were taking this serious and were in their cellar. They have a habit of sitting outside and watching the clouds. Mom assured me they were in the cellar and told me it was "spooky looking outside." The sirens were sounding and it was hailing so loud she could barely hear me. She added that Clay and Lakyn Smith had joined them as they had no basement. I told her to stay put and I would call her when it was all clear in a few minutes. The tornado hit about a minute after we hung up according to my mom.

She recalled later that the cellar doors had been ripped off immediately and that a wooden table leg came "shooting" down the stairs before the stairway filled with debris. Dad told her they had lost their house when water and insulation started filtering down to them. It didn't take long for the roar to pass and the digging out process to start. We found out a couple days later that Dad's backache was due to broken vertebrae he suffered while trying to lift some heavy materials from their escape route. Once outside, there was an "eerie silence" broken only by the sounds of water running down the street and smoke alarms going off in their destroyed neighborhood around them.

We were frantic with worry at home watching the news. We tried over and over to get through to the folks by phone. The news reported Greensburg had taken a direct hit and 60% of the town was gone. Then, a few minutes later, they said 95%. We were able to get through to Alan Myers who said, "His house was still standing but things looked really bad." He would try to stay in contact to tell us more. That was the last of our contact with anyone from Greensburg that night.

Pat, Adam, and I knew we needed to get to Greensburg as fast as we could. The phones were all ringing because people here knew we were from Greensburg and that our parents and friends still lived there. We'd been through a similar experience on April 21, 2001 when an F-4 tornado mangled 1/3 of Hoisington, including our house. We had an idea of how to help and of what might be needed. Our parents were going to need help. All those people were going to need lots of help. So, we threw rakes, shovels, flashlights, trash bags, a chain saw, blankets, extra shoes, gloves, and bottled water into our pickup and headed south. Kandi and Dean left Medicine Lodge. Diane, Mike and Tori left Buffalo about the same time as we left Hoisington. So, we should have all reached Greensburg about the same time. When we got to Great Bend, the sirens were going off and the police would not allow people to go through downtown due to the high water. We were forced to take shelter in a motel storm shelter with about a dozen other children and adults who were all experiencing this type of weather for the first time. They were scared! So were we! It sounded like the tornadoes were working their way up towards us.

I think it did us all good to help calm these people. It calmed us and took our minds off of Greensburg for a bit. Pat was keeping an eye on the TV. He was very disturbed with the reports coming from Greensburg. We sure wanted to be there instead of where we were but knew we didn't need to give our family more to worry about. This could not be happening again! What are the chances of a family having two tornadoes knocking them down? They had to be okay.

Finally around 3:00 a.m., Kandi called with the wonderful news that Heather had managed to get into town and find her grandparents in the Dillon's parking lot. They were safe, shocked but not injured (or so we thought). Kandi took them home with her. Diane, Mike and Tori made it as far as the folk's house on Walnut Street before getting a flat tire on their Hummer. Because they had OnStar, they were able to get the call that our folks were safe. They were also able to report that the place was in shambles. They changed to their spare tire and headed to Medicine Lodge as well.

We decided after hearing the great news and getting the all clear weather sign we would go back home and grab a couple hours sleep and a few more items we might need in the coming days. None of us were allowed into town the next day or the next so we spent some quality time together in Medicine Lodge as a very grateful family. We learned over those two days about the magnitude of the destruction in Greensburg. We also learned of the loss of lives, especially the loss of a wonderful family friend, Colleen Panzer.

When we were finally allowed in town, the tears flowed freely from us all as we drove slowly through town to south Walnut Street. Where was Walnut Street? We turn left after the Kwik Shop. Is that the Kwik Shop? The landmarks, houses and trees that were so familiar to us were all gone or destroyed beyond recognition. The mangled steel legs of the water tower served as our guide. And the house on the corner of Sycamore and Wisconsin streets that Pat, Krissie, Adam and I had lived in so many years was still standing. It was gutted and mutilated but still standing. It would be recognizable from the air in the next weeks to come because of its green roof. The Big Well Park, where half the town kids practically grew up, was a mess. The infamous wall was severely damaged.

The Simmons house was no more. All that remained was the center wall, a bathroom and a huge mess. We followed a trail of broken dishes and silverware to find their fifth-wheel camper where a church previously stood on the next block north. The car and pickup were destroyed and still there but the garage was gone.

Going home was going to have a different meaning from now

on. Although one by one, all of Melvin and Lena Simmons' kids and grandkids had moved, we all considered Greensburg home. And figured it always would be. We had been there since 1979. Most of our kids had been born there. Dad retired from the city and mom from the school there. Our roots were deep and our love for the town was too.

So, we did what had to be done. Brother Mike came from Arkansas so we were all there. Every kid and grandkid was there. So were a bunch of wonderful friends and volunteers. We saved what we could. We dug through mounds of smelly rubble looking for a ring, a purse, a photo, a bible, anything that was salvageable. Some items with special meaning were found and some were not. The most important things were found on the night of May 4, 2007, Mom and Dad. They are our glue.

The lots were cleaned, leveled, filled and eventually sold. The folks decided to stay in Medicine Lodge and bought a house there. Greensburg is rebuilding and looking great. Some folks are rebuilding and some have moved on. There are big plans and dreams for that little town. I believe it will grow! It will prosper! And it will be beautiful again! I will visit it and our friends there and be happy for them all. I will miss the Big Well Park, Hunter Drug, the siren that ran Monday thru Saturday at 7 a.m., 12, 1 and 6 p.m. and the first house that Pat and I bought. I will miss feeling like I am home.

submitted by: LOUIS A. TOMLINSON
116 E. BAY SHORE DRIVE • JACKSONVILLE, NC 28540

I Had a Home I Could Go To

This is a true story at the best I can remember it. I wish it was not because I lost the truck of my dreams and as my sister, Joanna, calls it, I lost my "go trailer". People ask me if I ever will recover or forget the night of the F-5 in Greensburg, KS, "I DON'T THINK SO"! But I did save my girls, Sammy and Boom-et. People ask me were you scared? There was no time to be scared, you had to act! I do believe that if you were scared and you froze, you were dead!

April 4, 2007 — I have been going to Kansas to fish and spend time with a good friend, Marvin Lawson. A couple years ago, my brother, Francis, came from Sacramento, California, and spent two weeks with Marvin and I fishing.

Living in North Carolina, I don't get to spend much time with family. I love my little brother and I do enjoy spending time with him. Over the past few months, we have been putting together another get together in Greensburg, KS.

It costs so much money nowadays to go anywhere; I just take my time and enjoy the trip. It took me 29 days to get 1500 miles, so I was in no rush.

First day on the road, I drove 200 miles to Badin Lake, NC where I always stop and do some fishing. It was cold and very windy so I only stayed two days. I packed up and went to my next stop which is the truck stop at exit 24 on Hwy. 40 west just past Ashville, NC. That was about another 200 miles a day and a stop overnight.

It was cool with a light sprinkle when I arrived there, so I checked my weather radio. It said the low the next morning would be 34 degrees and a light dusting of snow — NO BIG DEAL. (I have a heater).

The next morning I woke about 4:30 a.m. It was about 40 degrees in the trailer so I jumped up and turned on all three blocks on my propane heater and jumped back in bed till it warmed up. It took about twenty minutes to bust the chill and by this time Sammy and Boom-et (my pups) needed to hit the street. I got up and got ready to take them out. When I opened the door, there was about four inches of snow on the ground. It was 16 degrees and my truck was frozen shut. I walked down to the truck stop to get a cup of coffee and confirmed it was cold and still snowing.

It was now about 0700 and time to get off the mountain and into Tennessee and on into Kentucky where Sheila is at Fort Knox. I stayed a week with Sheila, TJ and Will, my new grandson. It is always uplifting to see my baby Sheila as we have lost a lot of good times together. I then headed out to Muskogee, Oklahoma to see Cpl. J.D. Mathews and his future wife, Tammy. (J.D. does not know this yet, but I would like to see it happen). I stayed about nine days with J.D.; he said to stay another week. Now, I wish I would have. However, I told Marvin I would be at his house on May 1.

May 2, 2007— I left J.D.'s and headed to Waynoka, Oklahoma to Harley Sullivan a good friend I had not seen in 32 years. Harley and I hung out together in high school along with Bob Russell (1964-1968). The last time I saw Harley was at Camp Pendleton, California, when I was with shore party in 1975. It was great to see Harley and talk about old times, and I look forward to seeing him again.

May 3, 2007 — I left Waynoka early in the morning and headed to Marvin's. I arrived in Greensburg, KS, at about 10:30 a.m. and let Marvin know by CB radio that I was in town. I topped off the truck with diesel fuel and went to Marvin's house. I was glad to see Marvin and Boomer and the girls were ready to run the yard. Marvin gave me the usual B.S. about taking a month to drive 1500 miles. We sat on the front porch and had a beer together while we watched the news. The day was cool and real nice for the girls to run. Marvin said they have been having weird weather; cool and wet. We goofed off the day and I went to the trailer to bed early.

May 4, 2007 — I got up early and had coffee with Marvin on the porch while we watched the news. The local weather report said a chance for heavy thunderstorms with large hail. It was no big deal as we have been through this before in western Kansas. Late afternoon, the report was we will have large thunderstorms and large hail. In early evening towards the southwest, we saw thunderstorms building. The storms, or I should say thunderheads, looked like an A-bomb had been detonated. They were huge mushroom clouds and very dark. You could see green in the clouds and that meant here comes the hail. I pulled the trailer up to Gary's stop as it was a closed down gas station to get the truck and trailer under cover. The gas station had a large cover over the pumps and I had parked there during storms in previous years. I walked back to Marvin's with the girls and Marvin and I checked on the storms off and on; on the weather channel. About 2100, the sky was really lit up with lightning, so I walked back to the trailer and truck with the girls. As I got to the truck, it started raining and rain came so hard it just roared on the awning. I opened the door on the trailer and the girls and I sat inside and watched the rain. At about 2120, Marvin called me on the radio and said there was a possible tornado on the ground southwest of Coldwater by the town of Protection which is approximately 28 miles from Greensburg. I switched the CB radio to National Weather Service and got the atlas out to possibly check the track. The tornado warning went off at 2130 and the news was putting out warnings every three minutes. 1st warning- 2133, the tornado was going to go west of Greensburg. 2nd warning- 2136, the tornado was going to go east of Greensburg. 3rd warning- 2139, the tornado has turned north and is going straight towards Greensburg and is picking up speed. 4th warning- 2142, the tornado is just south of Greensburg.

I put the girls in the truck and started backing out to run west on Hwy. 400. The hail started coming down and it was a little bigger than a golf ball so I hesitated and looked towards the Coastal Store south across the street. Just as I looked, there was a large lightning strike and I saw the tornado; it looked like it went from the East Coast to the West Coast. The rain and hail stopped then got dead quiet; no wind, no nothing.

I knew right then, we had it. I got the girls out of the truck and was running across the street to the Coastal Store when I heard what sounded like a fluctuating beehive with a slight whistle. As I got to the Coastal Store, I saw an eighteen-wheel truck fly across the road to the north. I turned to look at the truck and trailer and I saw my trailer just blow up. Just as I got in the store, (I was going to get in the freezer) all of the windows blew inside. The south wall came down and the roof caved in. As I glanced to my left, I saw two people duck in the womens restroom, so I ducked in the mens restroom. The restrooms were made of bricks and were my only chance. As I ducked into the southwest corner on the floor and I got the girls in my right arm underneath me, I wrapped my left arm around the base of the toilet. The door started slamming at the top and bottom. I turned to look at it, just as the door came off and flew straight up in the air. (It sounded like ice cubes in a blender). At about the same time the roof came off and sucked my wallet out of my pocket and almost took Boom-et out of my grasp, the south wall caved in on my back. I scrunched down so the toilet would take some of the weight and as I did the north wall came down on the south wall. Just as fast as somebody snapping their fingers, it was all gone. I was in the open and taking a beating, but I was not letting go of the dogs or the toilet. A big piece of plywood landed on my back. (My sister Joanna says our dad put it there). You name it and it came down and buried us. I don't know how long it was but I waited till I no longer heard a noise and it quit raining JUNK AND BOARDS. When I thought it was safe enough to dig myself and the girls out, at first I could not move around.

I moved a little here and a little there and got a hole big enough to crawl out of. When I got out, it was so dark I could not see much of anything. I was lucky to have grabbed a flashlight. It was like I was in another world that came out of nowhere, and it was. I had Sammy and Boom-et one under each arm and flashlight in hand going to the truck and trailer. The town of Greensburg was a large trash pile; eighteen wheeler trucks turned over, cars thrown everywhere along with lumber. It was hard to walk with all the lumber and nails sticking out everywhere you tried to go. I walked across the street to the truck and trailer and they were gone. I started looking around and then realized I was a block down the street from where I left them. The rain was coming down at a slant from the west. The gas station I was at still had a east and north wall still standing so I leaned up against the east wall to get out of the rain for a few minutes. I heard a slight whistle so I leaned over and looked around the corner to the northwest and saw a small tornado about forty yards from me chasing the big tornado to the northeast. I then walked a block up the street to the west to check on the truck and trailer. When I got there, the gas station was gone. The car, people parked under the awning because of the hail coming, was gone, too. I then saw the F-350 with all the windows blown out and the camper shell was also history. The place where the trailer was parked was an empty spot; frame and all gone. (Marvin and I found the trailer frame about two hundred yards to the northeast ten days later in a pile of trash). I started looking around for about fifteen minutes. There was nobody but me out on the street. I finally saw flashlights and heard people yelling for family and friends. I started for Marvin's house which was three and a half blocks away. Trash was blocking the streets and power lines were on the ground all over. There were people walking around crying and moaning, bloody and pretty well beat up. There was also people crawling out of upside down cars and cars that were thrown into what was left of houses. I got past the first pile of trash and I could not tell where I was at, so I walked back to Main Street. I had to somehow find out if I lost Marvin. I really didn't think he could have got out of what I was looking at. Rescue people were setting up flood lights so I figured I would make another try when I heard, "Hey Lou!!" Marvin came walking out of the dark with Boomer in his arms. We were beat but we were together and that was good enough for me.

This story could go on for another ten pages on how we were evacuated to hospitals and homeless shelters. Also, how we looked for three weeks for whatever we could find and recover. It was pretty much all gone.

The people in Greensburg, KS are all good people who lost everything from loved ones, animals, houses, vehicles, to livelihoods. I, at least, had a home I could go home to and I am thankful for that.

Thank you to J.D. Mathews and Tammy for coming from Oklahoma to the shelter in Haviland, KS. To: Harley Sullivan for offering to come to my aid. To: J.D. and Harley, I say SEMPER FI. To: Aunt Dorothy Roland and Daniel for taking me in for a month. A special thanks to Marvin Lawson for walking out of the nightmare with Boomer at hand. To: Aunt Blanch for selling me her van so I could get me and my girls, Sammy and Boom-et, home.

Swigart House   *Photo by Bruce Foster*

Prairie Point Apartment Complex   *Photo by Bruce Foster*

submitted by: SHIRLEY RICE

OLD ADDRESS: 417 CHERRY DRIVE • GREENSBURG, KS 67054
NEW ADDRESS: 307 W. SPRUCE, BOX 412 • MINNEOLA, KS 67865

God Has a Plan For All of Us

May 4th, 2007, was an ordinary day. I was preparing for a visit of two daughters for Mother's Day. The Beautification Committee had planted flowers in the mini-park and plans were being made for the Memorial Weekend. I thought the weather was strange when I heard thunder while the sun was shining. The black cloud came from the south, the storm warnings went off and the TV told us to take shelter. I went to the basement. The hail came and the house creaked like an old ship at sea. Within minutes, it was over. I went upstairs and found part of the roof blown off on the southwest part of my house as well as part of the garage roof, but because my builder, Doug Harrell, had put hurricane clips on the roof, my roof did not all blow away. Windows were out and the rain was coming in. All my fifty year old trees were blown down, but I was safe.

Neighborhood men came to see how I was. Someone came and suggested I go to the Conklin's as there were people there gathering. Mary Lou Schenk, the Conklin's and I spent the rest of the night waiting for the morning which we really didn't want to come. An eerie lightning continued through the night leaving shadows of the ruins. People from other towns worked all night clearing streets and looking for victims in need. Someone told us Main Street was gone. It was hard to imagine. About 6:00 a.m., someone came and said we were to go Dillon's to register with the Red Cross. Conklin's car was drivable so we drove to Dillon's. We drove around to see the damaged city and felt so sorry for what happened during the night to our beautiful town.

My brother and nephew had come to find me at 3:00 a.m. and could not find me because I was at the neighbors. They talked to someone who said they had seen me. They were relieved and went home to come back the next morning. My family and friends called the Red Cross but they hadn't kept track of me. The relatives suffered as they didn't know what had happened to their loved ones. We didn't know much of what was going on as we didn't have telephones, computers, or TV, so we were isolated. Neighbors helped neighbors, relatives walked into town and victims tried to find shelter. One EMT who came that night, said she gets a sick feeling when she comes into Greensburg remembering her experiences not knowing what they would find as a result of the tornado.

My entire family came to help me. They packed, took care of food, and cleaned the yard and anything that needed to be done. Friends stopped to see me and everyone was glad to see each other and know we had survived. We were thankful to God for his care and to those who prepared food, gave us water and encouragement. It gave us new appreciation for our fellowman.

Our lives have been changed. I spent one day thinking what I needed to do and where I should go. Monday, after the storm on Friday, I purchased a home in Minneola. I moved into it in June. I am living near my brother and other relatives. The people in the community have been kind. I feel I had lost my "identity" after having lived in Greensburg for fifty-seven years and I am forced to start a new life. I miss my friends, people I had known for most of my life, my activities and the town that was Greensburg; I know God has a plan for all of us.

submitted by: SANDY FOSTER

OLD ADDRESS: 122 W. GRANT • GREENSBURG, KS 67054
NEW ADDRESS: 10408 W. RIVER ROAD • PRATT, KS 67124

Our Faith Was Strengthened

May 3 was my husband, Brian Foster's birthday. We had made plans to surprise him on Saturday, May 5, by taking him to Wichita to the Warren Theatre to see, "Spiderman 3." So on Friday, May 4, I, our two grown daughters, Erica and Alyssa, our son-in-law, Brandon, and our two grandchildren, Kaylee and Jason, mostly had our minds on getting a few things packed for our surprise trip the next day.

We were all tired from a week of work; too tired to even become concerned about dinner. It was around 9:00 p.m. when Alyssa called and said that Brandon was watching the weather and they were coming over to be near our basement in case of an emergency. (They lived four blocks away from us in Greensburg.) After they arrived, Brandon turned on the weather report at our house and declared that the siren should be sounding very soon. No sooner he he said that, the siren blasted away.

We had been through the drill so many times, we knew to go obediently to the basement, but not believing that this time there would actually be a tornado strike, we did not take flashlights. We did, however, have a cell phone and a small digital camera. Taking pictures of our family sitting around in our basement became a way of entertaining ourselves minutes before the tornado hit. These pictures have become historic to us.

Suddenly, the phone upstairs rang our message machine went off with the voice of my friend Marilyn Rose nearly yelling, "Sandy, get into your basement! There is a mile-wide tornado headed straight for Greensburg!" I knew that her husband, Robin, must be out storm spotting and so we took this all very seriously.

We had lived in our 112 year old Victorian house for twenty years. Almost as though he were having a premonition, Brian had been investigating outside storm shelters for the last year. He had begun saying, "If a tornado ever hits this house, this basement will not hold out." I had put a damper on the storm shelter project because I told him that he could get the shelter for him and the rest of the family, but that I was too claustrophobic to ever get inside and shut the door.

So, after hearing Marilyn's voice, Brian was trying to think fast as to which part of the basement we should stay in for maximum safety. He decided that we should all go into the boiler room because it was smaller and had the boiler in it to hold up the roof. He would stay in the room closest to the outside door to dig us out. Fear was mounting in me with every minute that passed. We decided to light candles in case we lost power. Seconds later, the power, indeed, went out.

I looked over at Erica's face and her eyes were big. "Do you hear that?" she asked. I didn't hear anything where I was sitting. I became terrified of being buried alive in the basement as I saw her reaction to what she was hearing. My reaction was to jump up from where I had been sitting and yell, "No! It's alright!" (total denial) Erica knew it wasn't alright and she said, "I'm blowing out these candles!" I said, "No, no, no!" I knew we hadn't brought flashlights and that the darkness would make me more claustrophobic. As it turned out, it was probably better that we couldn't see what happened in the next few minutes, as it may have been more terrifying.

We all began praying at the top of our lungs. Erica was shielding her two-year old and was calling on God to save her baby. Brandon was sheltering Jason, who was only ten months old. Alyssa was calling out to God that if we were to die that He would safely see us through to his Kingdom. I was praying for Jesus to protect us, and wondered why I hadn't prayed earlier.

The next thing we knew the basement ceiling/upstairs floor was crashing in on us and the house was collapsing into the basement. I was foolish to stand up because something hit me very hard on the shoulder and knocked me hard to the cement floor to my knees. I

Brian and Sandy Foster House After   *Photo by Erica Foster*

found that I could not stand up nor could I move in any direction. It was pitch black and all I could do was listen to the cries of our children and grandchildren and hope that they would live. I heard Brandon and Alyssa cry out that something had struck them on the head and it really hurt.

The noise in the basement was deafening and I could not hear anything from my husband in the next room, so I screamed his name as loudly as I could. I heard a faint reply, "I'm ok!" But then the house lifted up off its collapsing foundation and moved to the north several feet and there were things flying around and falling into that basement everywhere, so I screamed his name again. Again, I heard a very faint answer.

Then the house came crashing back down and further collapsed the structure around us and over us and on top of us. There was so much debris, insulation from the walls, dirt, and who knows what else that fell in on us when the house landed that my sandals were literally torn off my feet. It felt like a truckload of dirt fell into my mouth and I began spitting and spitting to get rid of it. It was also in my eyes and nose. I screamed for the third time my husband's name and I heard again a faint, "Honey, I'm ok!" I could not believe my ears, because the noise coming from the room he was in made it sound like there could surely be no place he could be in to survive.

I was fifty-three years old at the time of the tornado and had felt

deep fear many times in those years, but I had never experienced terror like that night. I wasn't sure our kids were still alive at this point, but I knew that Jason was because he was screaming in terror. I tried and tried to get up from where I was stuck, but to no avail. Finally, after what seemed like forever, the noise subsided.

Someone yelled, "Let's take a head count!" I shouted, "I'm ok!" I heard one by one everyone else's voice say the same thing! It was still so dark and I was fighting a claustrophobic panic being unable to move and thinking that it might be hours before we were rescued. I never did show panic to my family, and I am very thankful to God for that because it would have only scared our grandkids more and would not have helped anything.

Brandon pulled out his cell phone, and managed to push into the room by the outside door where Brian was. He and Brian used the very faint light of his cell phone to see a little and clear out some space. I heard Brian's voice say, "Send one of the girls." I figured, well he's found a little hole, but not big enough for anyone to move through. What had happened was that the house had moved several feet to the north and sealed off the outside door leaving only a very small hole to crawl through.

The girls were struggling with screaming babies and so Brandon himself found the hole and managed to push himself through. He lost his trousers on his way out, but he was through! When I heard

Brian and Sandy Foster House After

Photo by Erica Foster

Where Erica and Alyssa Foster Took Refuge Waiting For Others to Get Out   *Photo by Erica Foster*

Brandon's voice on the outside yell, "I'm out!" I knew we would surely all be able to push through. Someone passed my grandson to me and my granddaughter and I passed them through to Brian. He was able to push them out to Brandon, but Kaylee sustained a long scrape where a nail got her tummy when she pushed through. The girls were next. I heard them cry out that the water heater was burning them as they went through from the boiler room to the next room. The inner wall of the basement had collapsed as had the boiler and water heater. The path through to the other room was so small that we all had to crawl right over the hot water heater and could not escape the hot water leaking out.

After the grandkids and girls were out, it was my turn. I still could not see anything in the dark, but Brian had freed me from my little corner where I was struck. So, I made my way over the hot water heater to him, and he guided me to the hole and pushed on me. It was very tight and I was fighting panic, but I knew I had to make it though. It seemed safer outside than inside. However, the minute I stood up on the outside I found that I could not breathe. I wondered if I was having a heart attack or something. What was happening was that we had come out into a furious wind such as we had never experienced before. It was literally taking my breath away.

The girls were standing outside cradling the babies and wondering how to protect them. It was raining very hard and they felt that the wind would surely pull the babies out of their arms. Brandon yelled over the noise of the wind that they should take refuge in the garage, but then lightning revealed that the garage had vanished. The girls disappeared into the night desperately seeking shelter.

I turned around and saw that Brian was struggling to get through the hole. He finally pushed every bit of air out of his lungs and came through! Brandon went on ahead to catch up with the girls. I was still struggling to breathe, but I knew we had to move on.

My feet became entangled in the overhead wires that had fallen to the ground. I was afraid of the electricity, but then realized that there was none. Brian asked me, "Do you have on shoes?" I told him I had lost them in the basement. He said, "You have no shoes! There are nails everywhere!" I was having trouble comprehending what he was saying, since I was so overwhelmed with trying to breathe and walk against the wind.

We made our way to the middle of Grant Street, but there was no place without boards and nails. However, I was not stepping on any nails whatsoever, and did not realize until later what a miracle that was. Brandon, Alyssa, and Erica had all lost their shoes in the basement also; they did not step on any nails either! We saw our kids out ahead of us, and knew they were ok, but then I heard Erica scream, "We're going to die!" She was afraid the wind was going to take Kaylee right out of her arms.

Brian clutched his chest and stopped moving. I was really frightened that something was seriously wrong with him. He told me to go on without him, but I told him, no way! He was actually alright, but he thought that he was holding me back, since he was having a lot of trouble walking against the wind. When we made it to the intersection of Grant and Walnut right beside the clinic, suddenly we heard the sound of a pickup door being ripped off a pickup! It made a loud noise while flying down the street. I was afraid it was going to smack right into us, but we could not move any faster in the wind, rain and hail to get out of its way. To our relief, it finally landed somewhere. We got a glimpse of the hospital in the lightning and saw that there wasn't much left of it. We made it to the north entrance and while we were wondering what to do next Chris Gardiner, one of our physician's assistants, and a handful of people approached us from behind. "I have a key!" Chris said. "The basement is storm safe!" He unlocked the door. The ceiling was falling into the hallway of the hospital, and I wondered if we could walk through it safely. It was very dark, but we made our way down the long corridor to the doorway of the basement.

When we arrived in the basement, the only light was a small, red emergency light blinking on the wall and sounding an alarm. With that little light, I could see with relief that the hospital staff had safely brought down all the hospital patients to the basement. Several people from town had also taken refuge there and were lined up in the hallway. We plopped ourselves down on the floor also, not knowing what else to do.

There was a man whose back had been injured in the tornado sitting in the restroom with the door partially open. He had his large dog in there also. Every now and then he would cry out in pain, but until he could be taken to a functional hospital there seemed to be little anyone could do to help him. I knew him so I tried to say something comforting to him, but felt pretty helpless.

Every now and then someone would be brought in on a stretcher to wait for an ambulance. I had a sense of dread that there would be many people seriously injured or deceased brought in, but in the dark I could not tell much. Our granddaughter was sitting on her mother's lap in a daze, not moving or speaking, and our grandson had fallen asleep in his daddy's arms. We sat like this for hours, and finally, Tish Smith, one of the nurses on duty that night, asked if any of us needed medical help. By this time, my back and knees were really hurting, so she gave me some pain medicine and decided that I and my whole family should be checked out in another hospital. I will always admire how she took care of everyone that night and remained so calm.

I kept saying, "Our families are going to hear about this and wonder if we're alive or dead!" That thought really bothered me. I could only imagine their fear when they heard. I kept trying to call them on my cell phone but there was no reception.

After another hour or so, we were escorted to a pickup to be taken to the triage at the Dillon's parking lot. We crawled into the back of it and took off. We were able to see a little bit of the city in the light of the car headlights, and were shocked beyond words to finally see what our town looked like. The pickup had to plow through trees and boards and lots of debris in the street as it made its very bumpy way down the road. Most of what we saw wasn't even recognizable to us.

As we arrived at the triage center, we saw many people from town walking around the parking lot in a daze. It was cold, and some people were huddled in blankets. Eventually, my family was loaded up into an ambulance and taken to Pratt. We were in the hospital gowns we had been given at the Greensburg Hospital to wear because our clothes were soaking wet, and that was all we had to our name; not

even any shoes. In the ambulance, I kept looking at our grandkids wondering if they were in shock because they were awake, but sitting so strangely still. I'm sure they were having a difficult time processing what had happened to them. Plus, it was the middle of the night.

My sister, her husband, and my nieces and nephews all lived in Hutchinson. As we found out later, my niece, Angie, and her husband, Steve, were sitting in a movie earlier that evening when both of their cell phones went off at the same time. It was my sister on one phone and Angie's dad on the other phone saying the same thing, "Greensburg has been hit by a tornado." Steve told Angie not to panic, the news might not be as bad as it seemed. They went home and listened to the television reports. They heard that the Big Well was destroyed; then the high school, then the hospital. That was alarming to them since we lived on Grant and Sycamore which was right in the middle of those places. Angie's biggest concern was that we were all watching a movie in our upstairs theater room and did not hear the siren go off.

My nephews decided that they were going to Greensburg, find our house and dig us out of the debris, if necessary. Their families were concerned about them running right into the same storm that hit Greensburg, but they could not be dissuaded. So Terry, Jeremy, and Jeremy's wife, Haleola, took off in their pickup with a promise that they would first stop in at the Pratt Hospital to see if we happened to be there.

As the good Lord would have it, our ambulance arrived at the emergency exit of the Pratt hospital at the same time my nephews arrived in their pickup. Jeremy's smiling face was the first sight we saw as we exited the ambulance, and it was so comforting! He was grinning from ear to ear and immediately called our family back in Hutchinson to report. He said to Angie, "You'll never guess who I'm looking at right now!" I am so very thankful to God for his timing. The agony our extended family had been in for hours came to an abrupt end as they realized we were all alive and well!

I was taken to a gurney to wait for my turn at the x-ray machine to make sure the pain in my back was not from a break. As I waited and looked around the halls of the hospital, I saw many people from Greensburg waiting their turn for a doctor. Some of them were extremely bruised with skin missing from their faces and arms. I felt so blessed to be in the shape I was in. The strange, faraway look on these people's faces broke my heart. I tried to talk to some of them, and some answered me, but it seemed as though they were in a trance.

My turn came for an x-ray. Dr. Cannata was very nice and gave me some strong pain medicine which helped so much. When I found out that the x-ray was normal, I laughed to myself for relief that I didn't have any broken bones to deal with. My family all checked out ok, though Brandon and Alyssa had bad headaches from being hit on the head.

All of my family and Brandon's family gradually arrived at the hospital; by this time it was the morning of May 5. Their faces were a welcome sight to our eyes! Brandon's mom, Pam, went to Walmart and bought us sweatshirts and pants and socks and shoes! Then my niece and nephews, and sister and brother-in-law took us to Hutchinson with them. It was so wonderful to have such a loving family gathered around us to help!

We checked in at a Hutchinson hotel, cleaned the filth off of us and got into bed. No one was able to sleep. I was learning what post-traumatic stress syndrome could feel like. Every time I closed my eyes, I was back in that basement in a panic again. I could hear and feel and taste the whole thing over again.

When we were allowed back into Greensburg a few days later, we were absolutely grief-stricken at the sight of our house and our town.

Our beautiful Victorian home was completely destroyed. Most of the house was reduced to what looked like mulch. What was left had indeed fallen into the basement. We stuck our camera into the hole we crawled out of and took a picture of the basement which revealed that miracles do happen. It looked like a place where no one could have survived, yet seven people did! It is truly a miracle.

The next few days were taken up with finding a place to live. There were seven of us homeless, since Brandon and Alyssa's house was destroyed also. That was five adults, two small children and three little dogs without a home. Brandon's father found us an unused parsonage in Sylvia, KS, for us to stay in for the time being; for which we were very grateful. After a few days, we realized that it would be too far to drive to work from there, so we began searching for another place.

A beautiful home in Pratt, that had just been built and was uninhabited, came to our attention. We knew how difficult it would be for our grandchildren to be unsettled for a long period of time. We made a decision to buy the house. In one day, we bought two cars and a house! We had never made such grand decisions in one day before! After a period of time, our grandkids began to feel settled and Kaylee would say with pride, "This is our new home! The old one went crash! Crash! But now we have a new one!" We knew from this that we had made the right decision, and we were glad that we were able to make it quickly.

We were able to retrieve a few things from the remains of our house, but not very much. My nephew, Steve, rescued our stove which was fairly new. It is a symbol of home to me, and I appreciate having it in our new home. We lost some very precious home movies, but we salvaged some too. Replacing every single thing we owned was overwhelming, but the great kindness and generosity of so many people who gave money to help the people of Greensburg made the task much easier. We are grateful beyond words to them and encouraged to know that there are still good people who care about others in this world.

A couple of people whom I cared about very much died the night of the tornado. I really believe that they died quickly and didn't have time to suffer much. Losing them was hard, but I have peace knowing that they are both in heaven. It took us the whole first year after May 4, 2007, to begin to feel normal again. I can now write this account of that night, whereas until now it has seemed too painful a task.

I still work in Greensburg at the Iroquois Center, as do Alyssa and Brandon. We no longer live there, but are rejoicing with every person who is rebuilding. Many people are receiving volunteer help, which is so good to see. I confess to still having sadness as I remember the way Greensburg used to be. I lived there most of my fifty-four years. But, I rejoice to see the city coming back to life and rebuilding.

Our faith in God was strengthened greatly by this experience. God's hand has been seen in our lives and in our town in so many ways. We thank him and appreciate all that he has done for us through this ordeal. There is so much suffering in this world we live in. Many people have suffered tragedies that make ours seem small by comparison. But one truth remains: even when life is hard, God is still good!

SUBMITTED BY: **HARLIN AND JEAN YOST**
OLD ADDRESS: 624 S. GROVE • GREENSBURG, KS 67054
NEW ADDRESS: 508 S. ELM • GREENSBURG, KS 67054

Clock Stopped at 9:44

The clock on the wall stopped at sixteen minutes until ten o'clock. Then the lights went out, the siren stopped and with flashlights in our hand and billfold in my pocket, we went to the storm cellar. It had a concrete top which proved to be a very safe place. Then the grim reality struck when parts of the house came down the cellar stairway. We knew that the house had given up to the 205 m.p.h. wind. Joe and Karen had stopped in because of the excess lightning, rain, and hail. While listening to the weather monitor, we knew the weather was very severe so we thought it best to get flashlights and prepare to get shelter. After the storm passed, Joe made his way out of the cellar and walked over to Aaron's house. That was about three blocks. Their home was standing with some damage. Joe returned and took myself, Jean and Karen to Aaron's, and then left to see if he could get to their house. It was possible, but very difficult with trash, light poles, wire,

dead cattle and traffic. He found their home in good condition. The storm passed east of their farm about ¼ mile to the east. Joe's pickup was very much damaged on the right side, but was yet able to drive it. However, he left it at the farm and brought his newer one to town and then took Karen, Jean, and I to the farm at 2:00 a.m. We slept well. The morning came and we continued to live with Joe's perhaps a week and then we went to live at Home Again for nearly thirty days. We were very fortunate to get a call from Ryan Penners and offered to sell their home to us. They were moving to Goshen, Indiana. Shortly after they left, some sweet sisters cleaned the house along with Karla, Angela, Jevon, Marijke and Ervin from Michigan as well as Joe and Karen and others in the family. We thank our heavenly Father for all the help, kindness, love and gifts that were given. We moved one more time to our present home at 508 S. Elm, Greensburg, KS.

66

2006 Picture of the Paul and Shirley Unruh Farm   *Photo by Shirley Unruh*

Gene and Margaret Bradley House Rebuilt   *Photo by Bruce Foster*

submitted by: **TOM AND KATHY DOHERTY**
OLD ADDRESS: 220 N. BAY • GREENSBURG, KS 67054
NEW ADDRESS: 506 S. GROVE • GREENSBURG, KS 67054

Getting Back to Normal

When I closed the Duckwall's store on May 4, 2007, I knew we were under a tornado watch. The weather was hot and humid, but the sky looked different. I figured we would probably get some rain and possibly hail, but I wasn't concerned. Tom was late getting home and we had a late supper. After supper, we decided to watch a western movie we had recorded. We weren't paying attention to the weather until we heard the siren going off.

I turned over to a TV channel to see what was going on and Tom went out on the front porch to see if he could see anything. They talked about the tornado on the ground between Coldwater and Kiowa County. I called my son, John, who lives in Bucklin; he always watches the weather on the computer. He said he had been watching it and it looked like it was going east of us. I told Tom what he said, but Tom couldn't see anything. We decided to get shoes on just in case. Then the lights went out and the siren stopped and Tom went back out on the front porch.

I was in the dining room getting out our flashlights when the phone rang. I had one phone that didn't run on electricity in my office right off the kitchen. When I picked it up, John was on the other end. He said the tornado made a turn and was heading straight for Greensburg. We need to get in the basement NOW. I called to Tom and told him John said to get in the basement that it was heading our way. We called Mac (our dog) and headed to the basement. Tom went to open the west window and the door that went outside on the north basement wall blew open or out, not sure which. Tom was blown up against the south wall and I grabbed the big steel pole in the middle of the room. Tom managed to open two windows and then made it over to me. He said we needed to get somewhere else, but I wasn't letting go of that pole.

I remember when I was younger in Fairview, Oklahoma there was a tornado. My dad was a big man and he had me with one hand and my sister with the other. It took all his strength to get us to the cellar. Our feet were flying up behind us as he was hurrying to get us to safety. If he had not held on, I don't like to think what could have happened.

I was afraid to let go of the pole. Tom pried my fingers lose and we went over to farthest east wall in the middle of the basement. We weren't able to get under the staircase due to the door blowing open; the wind was too strong. Our ears started popping and our dog ran back upstairs. We could hear the house being torn apart and glass breaking; it was a horrible sound and feeling. I remember telling Tom, "We are going to blow away and Mac has to be dead." He just kept telling me to hang on to him and he will hold me and not let me go. He says I started screaming until it got deathly quiet. Tom wanted to go upstairs and take a look. I tried to talk him out of it, but he said he would be back. He wasn't gone long, before my ears started popping again and Tom ran back down. Again, we went back to the east wall and huddled together. It seemed like forever, but I really don't know how long it was before it was quiet again.

New Homes

Photo by Bruce Foster

Tom said he thought it was over and we needed to try and get out. I wasn't so sure but he convinced me to go upstairs. He had to push real hard to get the door open a crack. There was so much debris in front of the door. We were able to squeeze through into the dining room. We were trapped right there. We couldn't get out the back or front. I started yelling for help. Two young men suddenly appeared; one came from the south side of the house, the other from the north side. They wanted to know if we were hurt. We didn't think we were hurt, just trapped. The one from the south said, "Here's a dog, is it yours?" We told him it probably was and asked if he was alive, he said "yes." We were so surprised; the young man picked him up and put him out on the ground. They moved enough debris to get us out; we had to climb over some stuff with their help. They helped us down to the ground. We heard one of my cats meowing, but didn't go find her at that time. I had another cat that always went outside. He would show back up about the time the tornado hit and eat some and then go out again. I figured he was probably at the back door when the storm hit. When we were able to go back to the house that night, we couldn't hear the cat in the house anymore, we figured she was dead or got out.

We never did find the cats, even though I checked two or three times a week with the animal rescue. They even put a trap on my property to no avail. In early February 2008, I was getting ready to turn on Hwy. 54 by the car wash. I noticed a cat lying in the field on the north side of the street. It looked like my cat that would have been outside during the tornado. I pulled across the highway and walked over to it. It had been hit by a car and was dead. I am sure this was our cat; the other cat never showed up anywhere.

The two men that rescued us told us to go to the hospital. We checked on the neighbors to the south of us and headed towards the hospital. It was dark and debris was everywhere; it was hard to walk. When we got up to Hwy. 54, there were several people. Some were in shock, some were panicking and others said there was another one headed our way.

We tried to tell them to go to the hospital, but they wouldn't listen. We decided to go on; we were having trouble finding out where we were at, due to all the damage. We came across a man who needed help getting his family out, so Tom went with him. I proceeded on to the hospital. I was just walking not sure where I was and started walking in water, in some places up to my knees. I couldn't figure where all the water was coming from; I never once thought of the water tower. I finally spotted some people in front of a building and I walked up to them and asked as if this was the hospital. They said, "yes" and this was all that was left. I stood with them awhile, but I felt like I was going into a sugar low (diabetic). I decided to find a curb and sat down over by the clinic. I don't know how long I was there or what took place, but the next thing I knew I was alone. Everybody who was there was gone. I didn't know where they went.

Then I heard Tom asking if anybody had seen his wife and calling my name. I couldn't see him so I called "Tom" several times and he finally heard me. He wanted to know where I had been and I said "here in front of the hospital." He had gone to the hospital basement and I wasn't there and nobody had seen me. He panicked and ran back where he had left me and kept looking for me all the way back to the hospital basement. When I still wasn't there, he was really getting scared. Then he heard me yelling. I didn't know I was to go to the basement of the hospital. I told him about my sugar and we went to find a nurse to get something for me. They asked for some help taking injured people to Dillon's parking lot and get them on the ambulance. Tom went to help; they were taking the people in the back of a truck. That is where our son, John, found him. He said he tried to call us again and when he couldn't get through he headed to Greensburg. They wouldn't let him in on the highway so he took dirt roads. He got stuck and someone else on the road pulled him out and was able to keep going. When he got to our house and seen the damage, he was hoping we were in the basement. When he couldn't find us, he started looking around and spotted Tom on the back of the pickup; he jumped on and came to the hospital. When he came in and I spotted him, I broke down and started crying and wondering what are we going to do. He told me, "Right now you are going to my place and we will work it out later." We went back to our house so he could try and find our medicine. Tom and John were up in the house and I was standing out front. I saw someone running towards me; it was my oldest son, Ed from Medicine Lodge, who had been looking for us. He and his wife, Stacy, and my brother, Terry, were with him. I was so happy to see them. That's all I wanted after the tornado was to see my kids. We have another son that lives in Missouri who couldn't make it down. We were able to talk to him on the phone. Ed was walking around and trying to find Mac (our dog) and spotted him under the neighbors van. It was sitting in our backyard. He wouldn't come out so I started to call his name and he finally came to me. He was shaking and scared. We found a leash and put it on him, but I think he would have stayed with us without one. He never let us out of his sight and his attitude was different so we didn't know what he would do. We finally decided to take him to a vet and have him checked out. He was traumatized like us, so they put him on Prozac for awhile. He finally got back to his old self. When storms show up, he knows it before we do and he is under my feet until it passes.

We spent most of that night in John's basement and the next night wasn't much better. When we finally got back to town and surveyed the property, everything was gone. What wasn't damaged from the tornado was soaked from the rain from the later storms. The house and both vehicles were totaled. Our garage was completely gone.

We stayed with John for a month and a half. Then we decided to get out on our own. We went to Pratt and stayed in a motel until FEMAVILLE was ready for us to move in. Since the state wants our land for the new highway, we had to buy a new lot. Our new house came in late February and hopefully it will be ready for us to move in soon. I am working part-time at the Big Well gift shop. Since Duckwall's said they were not rebuilding. Things are getting back to normal for us, just in time for the next tornado season.

submitted by: LARRY AND CARLENE SCHMIDT
OLD ADDRESS: 320 W. SCOTT • GREENSBURG, KS 67054
NEW ADDRESS: 10311 29TH AVE. • GREENSBURG, KS 67054

God's Hand Was There

Little did I know, that Friday morning of May 4, 2007, that before the sun rose so many peoples lives, including my families, would be changed forever. Friends would be gone and my beloved home town would never be the same. If I had known what was coming, would I have done anything different that day? Maybe, I would have lingered longer over my morning cup of tea on the back porch or my afternoon Pepsi at Hunter Drug, or just stood on Main Street and observed the daily activity of rural life. The day did not foretell what was to come; just another windy spring day. But early evening brought a heavy thick feel to the air and before long there were storm warnings on the television.

That evening, our friends, Lyndon and Denise Unruh called wanting to know what the TV was saying about the weather. I told them that it didn't look too good but it was far enough away, you just couldn't tell. As they didn't have a basement, they came over to seek shelter with us if it became necessary. Denise grew up in Pennsylvania. At our first meeting after their marriage, she questioned us about the tornadoes in this part of the country. Our reply to her was that we had lived here for sixty-five years and had seen several, but never been close enough to witness any damage! There would be laughter over this remark.

When they arrived, I was watching the radar on the computer and listening to the weather radio. I had already taken four big flashlights and a blanket to the basement and had my weather radio and cell phone in my pocket. While we visited, the weather started to look pretty nasty. The weather radio was talking about the tornado's location north of Coldwater and giving details about its path. The computer radar did not look good either. I remarked that if the tornado didn't start to veer east that we were in big trouble. The last time we looked at the computer radar it looked like a picture of a hurricane, not a tornado. I had never seen anything like that on the radar before. The weather radio said that the storm was about one mile east of Hwy. 183 and seven miles south of Greensburg. Our farm was four miles south of town so we knew exactly where the storm was. All of this time, Larry had been watching the weather from our south porch. We lived on the first street on the south edge of Greensburg so he had a good clear view. He called to the rest of us and said he thought it was time to head to the basement. Lyndon, Denise and I proceeded for the basement and Larry decided to take one last look out the north door. Just as he did so, the wind abruptly switched to the north. He yelled at us to run and he followed. I was talking to our daughter, Carla, on the phone. She wanted to make sure we were watching the weather and to check on Machelle. I had just told her that her sister and her family were out of town when the phone and the electricity both went off.

In the basement on the northwest corner, we had an area that jutted out by itself under the back porch. This was where we decided to go in case of a storm. From that moment, it was as if things were in slow motion for me. When the storm hit, I could hear glass breaking and furniture scooting around upstairs. The sound was similar to a loud freight train. Then as quickly as the storm hit, it suddenly got deathly quiet. Then just as quickly as it stopped, it hit again only this time it was different. We were all praying but even as close as we all were you could barely hear one another. The noise was unbearably loud; like some evil, demonic, unearthly thing. We were all commenting about how our ears were popping. I knew at this point that the house was gone, but that as long as the floor above stayed intact we would be okay. Frequently, I would look up at floor joists and each time I did Larry would be looking up too. I never noticed any movement in the joists but there was one chink in our safe place; a small window on the north. I kept glancing at it too. Once when looking up, a water line that went through the basement wall to an outside hydrant was being pulled through the wall like a piece of spaghetti until it snapped off. The next time I looked up the window looked like a living, breathing thing and I remember thinking that if that window goes we are in trouble. I grabbed the blanket and rolled it around my forearms and crossed them over the window and ducked my head. As I stood there feeling the window pulsating, I prayed for the window to stay in place and thought that if this window goes, you are toast. Suddenly, it quit moving and I returned to the floor.

After it became quiet outside, we went up to survey the damage. The house was gone as we expected. Frightening to us looking north with the lightning flashing, we realized the water tower was gone and few structures left standing. Shortly, the neighbors began to gather, checking on one another. It was then that Denise and I thought we could hear someone yelling for help. I stepped back from the others to listen and could tell it was coming from the east. When I looked toward John Unruh's house, there was nothing and my heart sank. Larry, Lyndon, Denise and I took off in that direction. As it turned out, John and Elsie were okay but the stairway was gone and they couldn't get out of their basement. While the men were trying to help them out, I could hear someone else yelling for help. Looking again to the east, I could see that Trent's house was also gone and that the voice was coming from there. Lyndon and Denise stayed to help John and Elsie while Larry and I went on to the Trent's. We could hear the cries but it was so dark even with the flashlights; we couldn't find the person. Larry kept telling them to keep shouting as we were trying to find them. In my flashlight beam, I spotted two pair of blue eyes very close to the ground. I kept my beam on them and called to Larry as I knew they had two small dogs and that the dogs would be where their owners were. Sure enough, they were there. Their daughter was calling for help. Larry helped her to the road and told me to wait there and try to get more help. He returned to Danny and Saleena who were trapped under the remains of their home. He worked for some time before other neighbors came and joined in. They worked for some time moving debris. When to the west, I could see flashing lights. It was an ambulance crew from Coldwater. I hurried to their location and told them that we had people trapped under a house. It took some time for them to free the couple. Larry told me as we returned to our house that

Danny had never responded to him and that he really feared for his life. Saleena did talk to him even though she was severely hurt also.

Our daughter, Machelle, checked on us and said they were going to Dodge City for the night. I told her to please call Carla as soon as she could and let her know that we were okay. Larry and I decided that we would spend the night at our farm south of town. However after getting a few miles south of town, we could tell that the tree line at the farm was totally different. We knew that the storm had struck there too. We went back to town and spent what was left of the night in our basement. Later, the girls asked why we didn't just go to Dodge. I guess we both felt the need for one last night in the home we had built together before saying goodbye to it and a whole way of life that we knew was changed forever.

We are so thankful that all of our family was safe. Even though there were deaths from the storm, you could see so many ways that God's hand was there.

submitted by: JOHNNY AND JANET COCHRAN
OLD ADDRESS: 605 S. BAY • GREENSBURG, KS 67054
NEW ADDRESS: 323 SUNNYDELL CIR. • S. HUTCHINSON, KS 67505

"Stuff" Means Nothing

I am living in a small community in South Hutchinson, Kansas. Johnny's health precluded us from rebuilding in Greensburg. I am always thrilled to hear of the great progress being made there.

We took shelter under the stairs to the basement with a piece of paneling held to the opening. I felt the cement wall shake. We learned later the walls were very badly cracked. The house was standing but was not repairable. It was ours from the architect to the bulldozer. I don't think too many people could say that after forty-seven years.

Johnny was airlifted to Wichita as he was having difficulty with his health problems. Then in January 2008, his pacemaker failed and he passed out downtown, fell and broke his hip. After five weeks of inpatient care, he was doing pretty good but then his health deteriorated further and he passed away on August 6, 2008.

One thing still sticks in my mind after all this time. Our neighbor, Pearl Shank, came to my door the morning of May 4 and asked me to put her mail and newspaper in her door while they were out of town. She gave me her cell phone number and said, "If my house blows away, call me." Well, her house blew away and I didn't have phone service to call her. I told her to never say anything like that again!

I really don't think we could have made it without our family and friends. My mind was foggy for several months and I hear the same from others. I learned that "stuff" means nothing. Sometimes, I will look for an item but then realize I don't have or need it. I look back and am thankful for the years we all had together.

Mennonite Church   *Photo by Bruce Foster*

submitted by: **W.E. STEWART**

OLD ADDRESS: 405 S. GROVE • GREENSBURG, KS 67054
NEW ADDRESS: 1500 E. 6TH ST., BLDG A, APT. 1 • PRATT, KS 67124

Hasn't Been Easy to Move

On the evening of May 4, 2007, I went to an Odd Fellows #98 meeting at Pratt at 8:00 p.m. I'd been a member of this organization for sixty years. The meeting lasted around an hour. I headed home slowly as to avoid hitting a deer. I turned the radio on. They said that severe storms were at the Clark and Comanche counties moving northeast. I ran into rain at Cullison. The further west I traveled, I ran into hail and rain at Wellsford and Haviland. Past Haviland, the hail got larger and it put small dents in the car but didn't damage the windshield. About one and a half miles east of Greensburg, the rain came down in sheets and I could barely see. There was lots of lightning, wind, and thunder. I drove past the curve in Greensburg and noticed there were no street lights. I thought to myself that the electricity must be out. The further I drove the worse the debris was. At the corner of Hwy. 54 and Cedar Street, there was a highline pole in the street. Then a Highway Patrolman stopped me. I rolled my window down and talked to him. He explained there had been a tornado come through about five minutes ago and that there was another one coming. Sure enough, right on cue, the second tornado came. It came with a vengeance; the wind rocking my 1995 Buick car. I was scared it was going to tip it over. Then, it instantly stopped.

Knowing that the pole was interfering with my traveling further, I sat there and put my thoughts together. Within fifteen minutes, the Kansas Department of Transportation (KDOT) moved the pole. I proceeded west till I got to more debris. Then I parked the car and started walking to my house. The house was badly damaged; windows blown out, part of the roof gone, bricks laying on the ground, etc. The building of the house started on March 3, 1956, and my family moved in September 13. I have since sold the house to someone who is in the process of repairing it. A Highway Patrolman came along and said it was too dangerous for me to be here. He told me to go to the Coastal Mart and wait to be picked up and transported to KDOT. From there, they were taking people to Haviland on the bus. I decided that wasn't what I wanted to do. I had an obligation the next morning to be at Coldwater and help at the health fair. I made the decision to sleep in my car. I went to the fair and was back in Greensburg around 11:00 a.m. I went to the house again and was told again by the Highway Patrolman that the entire town was evacuated for search and rescue reasons.

I then spent the next two and a half weeks at the Haviland Shelter. The count went from one hundred persons down to twenty. Then I was transported to the Mullinville shelter and spent four nights there. I then went to Kingman and spent many nights in a motel room and traveled to Haviland and Pratt for meals. The day after Memorial Day I moved into an apartment at Pratt and lived there for thirteen months. In July 2008, I moved to another apartment.

It hasn't been easy to move to another town after living in one all your life. I go back quite often to Greensburg but it's not the same place. I continue to sell Watkins and Fuller Brush Products.

submitted by: **PEGGY KYLE**

729 W. MORTON AVENUE, UNIT 11 • GREENSBURG, KS 67054

Changes Still a Difficult Concept

The night of May 4, 2007, I was watching TV when the meteorologists were announcing the bad weather moving in our direction. I had decided to take a shower, get dressed for bed and watch more TV. After awhile, I figured I had better get dressed in regular clothes just in case I needed to move to shelter. I live in the Elmore Heights Apartment Complex which does not provide a storm shelter. The ironic thing about it is that the manager at the time inquired at the Carriage House Assisted Living Complex, across the street from my facility, of using their basement for shelter. (She just asked days before the tornado). When I was almost dressed, the sirens started to blow. I called Carriage House first to see if I could come over. Their answer was YES!

I gathered in their commons room and watched TV while it was raining and hailing outside. Then the residents were told to proceed to the basement. Everyone used the elevator except me. One man refused to leave his room. Once in the basement, there wasn't enough chairs for everyone so I stood.

Then my ears popped and I heard glass breaking. It was scary not knowing what was happening or what was going to happen. The residents didn't realize the severity of the storm. I'm not even sure they knew why they were in the basement. I waited awhile before thinking it was safe to go across the street. I borrowed a flashlight and slowly walked to my destination. My van had the windows blown out and a big dent on the passenger door. I arrived at the apartment. Everything seemed to be okay, so I spent the night in the apartment. It was hard to sleep as I was worried about the destruction of the rest of the town.

The next morning a resident came by knocking on my door and told me we were to vacate the premises with as few belongings as possible. That's when Ted and Linda Kyle, my brother and sister-in-law, showed up and said I was going home with them. I broke down and said, "Did you see my van?" Ted said, "Its just stuff!" I took some clothes and my medication. We drove through town pass the high school, hospital and other people's houses. Eventually, we drove up to our family home. SHOCK! It was unrecognizable. It looked like a big heap of rubble. Linda took pictures of it. So sad! Our father built the house when Ted was a baby; approximately sixty years ago. The east part of the house was added on when I was a baby in the era of the 1960's.

I lived with Ted and Linda for six weeks. After that time period, I moved back into my apartment. The apartment complex had roof damage and nicks and gouges in the siding. All the residents came back to occupy the facility.

Even though I was settled back into my familiar surroundings, the rest of the town was still in shambles. There were volunteers and residents still cleaning their lots, businesses and church properties. With all the debris being hauled off, the streets became detrimental with nails. I spent many hours at the tire shop getting my tires fixed.

Even though it has been well over a year since that fearful night, Greensburg would be forever changed. A part of me will always remember the Greensburg the way it was. I'll always remember the houses in town where my friends lived. I'll always remember the buildings on Main Street that had been there since Greensburg was established in 1886.

Greensburg is a generational town for the Kyle family. My father and his siblings were born and raised on the farm. My siblings and I were born and raised in Greensburg. My nephew and nieces were born and raised here. Plus, we are all Greensburg High School graduates.

I love Greensburg. Even though seeing the changes everyday is still a difficult concept to grasp, I know that God was with the people of Greensburg on the night of May 4, 2007.

submitted by: MARVIN LAWSON
OLD ADDRESS: 207 N. SYCAMORE • GREENSBURG, KS 67054
NEW ADDRESS: 517 E. NEBRASKA • GREENSBURG, KS 67054

I'm Not Dying This Way

I moved to Greensburg in the year 2000. I bought the house on 207 N. Sycamore on Christmas Eve. The house was in bad shape and should have been bulldozed down. However, my friend, Lou, came from North Carolina and helped me get it back together. That's the first time I've ever seen anybody camp on the inside of a house; I had no water or electricity. I cooked on two camp stoves and made a make-shift table to work on. By boiling water and making a five gallon bucket portable shower, I got by with what I had. It's amazing on what you can invent when the times are tough.

Lou comes back to Greensburg every year to see me. Our highlight of him visiting is when we go fishing and camping. Just like two typical ex-marine buddies, we get together to tell war stories and drink beer. I had my refrigerator, located on the porch, stocked with plenty of chicken and beer. He arrived in town on May 3.

On May 4th, we were sitting on the porch, feeling relaxed, and then the sirens went off. We'd been watching the radar on TV but it didn't look severe. How many bad storms hit Greensburg? Usually, everyone sits outside and looks at it. Lou said he thought he'd move his pickup and trailer underneath Gary's Stop Filling Station. I told him to go ahead and I'd be waiting for him to return. He no more left when the electricity went out and I lit a candle. I walked through the house and went back to my shop on the backside of the house. I shut the doors and made sure everything was in order for the night. I came back through the house; it was shaking a little, and I sat on the front porch. The cat, Goldie, was acting funny as she went under the couch. Okay,

she's safe! I closed the front door and the door fell on the floor. Then it felt like someone had pushed me down. The next thing I knew a wall fell on top of me. I don't know how long I was pinned. The rain poured down on me so fast that I had to use my caps bill to keep water from entering into my ears. I laid there with emotional anguish because I couldn't move. I told God, "You missed me in Korea, you missed me three tours in Vietnam and by gosh, you missed me again. I'm not dying this way and you better send someone to get me out of this mess. I am mad!" I punched my fist through the sheetrock wall and broke glass. Next thing I heard the neighbor kids hollering for me. They yelled, "Where are you?" I'm screaming, "I'm over here! Look for my hand waving at you!" I hear them walking through the debris. Then I exclaimed, "Get off of me! You are crushing me!" They uncovered me from the destruction and I stood up and said, "Good Lord, what planet am I on?" You talk about the TWILIGHT ZONE. I didn't recognize anything. My shop was gone. All I saw was bare ground; it picked everything up and swung it. The little angels I carry with me in my truck was holding that wall down on me; protecting me. All the angels were busy that night! How fortunate can I get!

Neighbors were helping neighbors. Everyone was concerned about the welfare of others. Mark and Kent Trummel helped me get Betty Hogan, my neighbor, out of her basement; her floor was gone. She was sitting down there in her rocking chair with a blanket around her. The guys guided us down the block to a cellar; it was full of women and I was the only man. I told them I couldn't stay as I

Marvin Lawson House Before   *Photo by Low Tomlinson*

had to find Lou. I was on my way back to my house when I found Boomer, my dog. He looked like he'd been rolling in the mud; his eyes were matted shut. I looked to the west and I saw lights. Other people were roaming around and they asked me if I was ok. About that time, I saw a bald-headed old man standing there with his two dogs under each hand. I hollered, "Hey, Lou!" He said, "Yo, Marvin! Oh Lord, you're alive! I was looking over there and didn't see you. I assumed you bit the dust." I said, "No, not yet! It's hard to keep an old Marine down. We might get knocked down, drug around, but, we get up, shake the dust off and keep going!"

Marvin Lawson House After   *Photo by Low Tomlinson*

The rescue personnel took us to the Haviland shelter. We were there for two days with me sitting there in wet overalls; with no change of clothes. They gave us two blankets each; one to lie on and one to cover up with. We had our three dogs with us. Someone in authority told a church lady that you must tell them they have to get out of here with those dogs. The lady said, "No way! They are two retired ex-Marines. They lost everything but the clothes on their back and those dogs." Eventually, we ended up in Ford with Aunt Dorothy and stayed with her a month. In time, we got ourselves re-organized with all the paperwork

I started looking for a house in Greensburg. I talked to my friends, Rex and Shirley Butler. They suggested a place for sale and so

I bought it. Ever since, I've been fixing it up and making it livable for Boomer and I.

I'm very fortunate to be alive. I'm seventy-two years old, not ready to go yet as I have too much to do. I retired from the Marines after putting in twenty years of service as a chef for the Generals. I met Lou through the citizen band radio talking on our, "Morning Show" in Jacksonville, North Carolina. I met him in person one year later and we've been friends ever since.

All I have is time! I want to see if they get this town built back up. God missed me this time and the next time he better get me good! I ask him everyday as to what plans does he have for me today!

submitted by: SHERI TAYLOR
OLD ADDRESS: 412 W. IOWA • GREENSBURG, KS 67054

God's Protection

Friday night, May 4, 2007, will forever be etched in the memory of the people of Greensburg and all of Kiowa County. It is amazing, even now, how a sound, a smell or a certain feeling can just instantly take me back to that night. It all comes back like it was happening all over.

For me, it was a typical Friday of work and then coming home to do my mowing and yard work before the weekend. I was so busy getting things done up before it got dark that I was unaware we were

under a storm watch. I got things all put in the garage and went into the house. When I a received a phone call that we were under a tornado watch. I didn't think too much about it until the sirens went off. I decided to round up some important papers, a couple of pillows, and a flashlight and head to the basement just in case. The longer the sirens lasted, the more serious I took the warnings. I ran upstairs a couple of times to grab important things. The last time

Sheri Taylor House After

Photo by Sheri Taylor

up, I remember how strangely hot and heavy the air felt. I went back down and got in my corner and was on the phone with my friend, Ray, when the electricity went off. The first thing I heard was the wind came up and my barbecue grill falls off the deck. The next thing I heard was glass breaking, hail hitting on the floor above me and the sound of boards ripping apart. At that point, I started having boards and debris come down on top of me pinning me down to the stool I was sitting on. I felt like I was slowly being crushed under the weight of the wreckage. As things got quiet, I realized I couldn't move, and I felt a cool breeze around me. Then, once again, the wind came on strong and blew again. I wasn't sure what I thought had just happened because I never did hear the train sound like people say you have with a tornado. As all of this happening, I was praying so loud for God's protection over me. I guess I couldn't hear anything else.

I am very claustrophobic. When I realized I couldn't move, I started to panic. I got a grip and realized if I panicked, I was in trouble! I prayed for God to calm me down. Then, just an unexplainable peace came over me. I could hear people in the distance hollering and someone calling my name. No matter how loud I yelled, no one could hear me. I decided I better save my voice. When I heard people real close, I could yell some more. Finally after a couple of hours, Ray led a rescue team to the corner of my house where I was under the rubble in the basement. He knew where I was because he had been on the phone with me right before it hit. The rescue team used chain saws to cut the boards above me and made a hole to pull me up and out. They grabbed me and carried me off to a pickup that took me to the Kansas Department of Transportation. I never looked back at my house to see what was left.

I don't think it actually hit me that my house was smashed flat until we went back in on Monday. That is when I became aware how much God was protecting me and many, many others on that Friday night of May 4th.

submitted by: **SHARON SCHMIDT**
OLD ADDRESS: 722 S. GROVE • GREENSBURG, KS 67054
NEW ADDRESS: 410 S. PINE • GREENSBURG, KS 67054

Humble, Heartfelt Thank You

One of the definitions of "recovery" according to the Webster's Dictionary is "regaining of something lost, balance, etc." While thinking back on how to summarize "recovery" as a family and community, it isn't very hard to see how the bad memories are by far outweighed by the memories of so many good deeds done by so many. This included the President of the United States.

In the eighteen months since the storm, I have discovered that as a person and as part of a community, it is possible to adapt to many changes. Some were temporary, some are permanent. Regardless of what change was occurring, it has been abundantly clear that God has never forsaken us, even in our most overwhelming of days. For this, I am grateful.

Since May 4th, 2007, my family and I have moved six times. The final move was to our new home at 410 S. Pine Street. What a day that was! The mud was ankle deep at Femaville as we moved out of our trailer and into our new home. Rain couldn't put a damper on the excitement of this move!

August and September of 2007 brought two surgeries for me. With the help of family and friends, these recoveries went well. August also brought a new school year for Taylor. It was a terrific feat to get this temporary school set up and started on time. The kids and staff have been incredible with this set-up. There have been days of high winds, hard rain, and snow leaving them uncomfortable at best.

December 19th of 2007 brought the birth of my first grandchild, Ryker. My son, Morgan, and daughter-in-law, Jateice, had told me the night of the tornado as we were walking through debris that they were expecting a baby, trying to put some good news into an overwhelming situation. Ryker has turned one year old and is such a blessing!

The New Year brought the beginning phases of our new home being built. It was so exciting to go over to see who was working there everyday, and watch the progress.

May 4th, 2008 brought not only the first anniversary of the storm, but my daughter's birthday and graduation from Southwestern College in Winfield with a degree in nursing. This was such a happy and proud day! We had special T-shirts printed up with, "Happy Birthday Tornado Ali." She shared her graduation day (and family) with the President of the United States. This was his second trip to Greensburg since the tornado and what an honor it was for these students to have him hand their diplomas to them!

August 2008 brought a new school year. Taylor started his senior year and is exploring his options of college's after graduating.

September 2008 brought a phone call from Ali's boyfriend, Jason, asking me for my blessing in asking for Ali's hand in marriage. Exciting plans are currently underway for their April 25th wedding at Greenleaf Ranch.

While this briefly tells of our months of "recovery," I would like to digress and share some of the no less important happenings during the days, weeks, and months following the tornado —

Memories spent in lines waiting to sign up for FEMA, Salvation Army and Red Cross; getting a tetanus shot from nurses who were walking up and down the streets of Greensburg with a shopping cart so that we would be protected; sights and smells never before imagined in our peaceful, small town; the National Guard lined all the way up north Bay Street and the media lined up on north Main Street made a surreal backdrop with planes and helicopters circling overhead; and shopping at the Salvation Army store located at an old grocery store in Pratt.

The community of Greensburg came together during these times, and it was so exciting to run into people from "home" that you knew. There was always a hug, and the question, "Where are you staying?" When Femaville opened for people to move into, there was once again a sense of community. We endured blowing dirt, blowing wheat straw, rain and storms that sent us to the storm shelters. Even though it was a temporary home, we were grateful for the comfort of being close to friends and family.

Words can not express the humble, heartfelt thank you to so many

that brought comforts needed. The caring, helping hands from all over the country are so deeply appreciated. Taylor and I have made friends with people from both coasts and everywhere in between. The names and best wishes of the people who worked so hard to get us into our house are written on a wall in our basement. It is a cherished souvenir that will never be covered!

May God deeply bless all those who came and donated their time and money.

submitted by: **JOHN AND JANICE HANEY**
OLD ADDRESS: 122 W. IOWA • GREENSBURG, KS 67054
NEW ADDRESS: 16472 B. STREET • GREENSBURG, KS 67054

Thank You Lord For Saving Our Lives

It has been twenty-one months since we wrote our last story. What a roller coaster ride! With every new day, we awake with a new challenge. We ask God what is his plan for us today. You know he won't give us more than we can handle. However, there are days we wonder if our cup is full up. It seems everyone in the community has had their share of struggles.

It was a joyous day when we got to move into our home on April 18, 2008. The house is built on the 100 year old farmstead established by John's grandfather, W.C. Mitchell. Our grandchildren

are the fifth generation to live in the original two-story farmstead house. With this heritage, we decided to get back to our roots. Our house is located one-eighth of a mile from this structure.

We chose to build an earth, berm home that has dirt pushed up on the east and west sides and the north and south sides have windows and doors. It features Low E-2 insulated windows, three foot roof overhang, ICF eco-block walls, geothermal heating and cooling system, cement roof, and radiant heated floors. Because we wanted to live in the house as long as possible, we have no basement

John and Janice Haney House Before   *Photo by Janice Haney*

John and Janice Haney House After
Photo by Janice Haney

or steps. Our safe room is a combination room of an office, laundry and bathroom. It is completely cement on all four walls, floor and ceiling. Our house is tornado proof. It's such a solid structure that we don't hear the wind blow or can not receive the cell phone frequencies. The water coming out of the geothermal system is emptied into a pond used for wildlife habitat and permeates back into the water table. Someday, we hope to add wind generators for a self-sustainable building.

Our lives have been changed forever. The things that were important before have no meaning to us now. We have decided to make our lives simpler. Our yard requires little maintenance. We are utilizing the habitat of native grasses and plants (little mowing needed), and planting a garden of flowers, vegetables and herbs. We are introducing the green initiative into our lives. It's amazing how we've always done these things but never thought it to be eco-friendly. We always thought it was a way of living on the prairie;

never thought any differently. I'm sure we all do them. The small things of life formulate our simpler being but big events are few and far between. It's the little things that make life worth living. Enjoy the great environment that God has so preciously molded on this earth. Don't take life for granted! As we all know, life can be changed and taken away from us in an instant.

The things we have discovered from our episode are keep copies of important documents in two places, put together a survival kit in your house, have a safe room in your home, have a disaster plan for all involved in your household, report to the Red Cross as soon as possible after a disaster, give generously to the Salvation Army and update your insurance frequently.

There are numerous stories that still need to be told. The main thing is that those who walked away from the destruction on May 4, 2007 are true survivors. You sustained a tremendous tragedy. Thank you Lord for saving our lives!

John and Janice Haney's New House
Photo by Janice Haney